Praise for
Type 1 Teens

Whether you are a teen with type 1 diabetes or a health professional who works with them, I absolutely recommend that you read *Type 1 Teens*. Dr. Hood's book offers a treasure trove of positive, constructive, and helpful ideas that meet teens where they are, and it is written in an engaging, conversational style. This book is an accessible and practical guide that teens, and the adults around them, can return to whenever the going gets rough with diabetes.

Tim Wysocki, PhD

Pediatric Psychologist, Nemours Children's Clinic, Jacksonville, FL

Dr. Hood has done an excellent job of combining research, clinical experience, and his own personal experience with diabetes to create a valuable resource. This book is user-friendly and addresses the most important topics for teens with type 1 diabetes. The exercises offer opportunities for teens to sort out how they feel about their diabetes and how to address problems that are unique to them. A must read for all teens with type 1 diabetes.

Michael A. Harris, PhD

Associate Professor, Pediatrics, and Chief of Psychology, Child Development and Rehabilitation Center, Oregon Health & Science University

----

Type 1 Teens is an essential book for adolescents of all ages with type 1 diabetes and their parents. This is the first guide I have seen which helps teens to problem-solve some of the toughest sticking points of living with diabetes in the adolescent years—how to negotiate with parents, how to solve problems involving peers, including dating, how to build and then help an "essential support roster" and an "expanded support roster". Dr. Hood provides a step-by-step practical guide to helping teens to own their diabetes, to advocate for themselves, and to recognize and manage early signs of "diabetes burnout". This book honestly speaks to the everyday dilemmas that come up in the lives of teens and how diabetes may complicate normal life happenings!

Barbara Anderson, PhD

Professor of Pediatrics, Baylor College of Medicine

Type 1 Teens is a must-have guide for teenagers (and their parents) dealing with the challenges of type 1 diabetes. Covering topics so important to the life of the teen—school, friends, parents—and tackling thorny issues, such as sex, drugs, and depression, this book is written in an informative and non-judgmental style that will keep teens engaged, help them understand their feelings, and provide the necessary tools to gain more control over their diabetes.

Stuart A. Weinzimer, MD

Associate Professor of Pediatrics, Yale University School of Medicine, Medical Director, Children's Type 1 Diabetes Program

----

Finally! A book about real life with diabetes for teens, a book that explores the hassles of living with diabetes (dealing with parents, feeling burned out, making new friends, and more) and provides simple, powerful solutions. Sure, diabetes isn't easy for teens, but it doesn't have to be impossible. And thanks to Dr. Hood, one of the leading experts in our field, and his wonderful new book, it may now become a little easier.

William H. Polonsky, PhD, CDE

Chief Executive Officer, Behavioral Diabetes Institute, Associate Clinical Professor, University of California, San Diego

----

Getting a diagnosis of insulin dependent diabetes triggers major coping issues for anyone. Add adolescence to the mix and stress levels zoom through the roof. Traveling the road to adulthood and establishing autonomy is hard enough without doctors, parents, and your own body reminding you of your vulnerabilities. Dr. Hood has done a fabulous job of bringing together the need-to-know essentials in a way that makes sense to teenagers and supports active positive coping. The book brings educational information and psychological strategies together in a uniquely powerful form uniquely suited to helping *Type 1 Teens* master and triumph over diabetes.

Gerald P. Koocher, PhD, ABPP

Dean and Professor, School of Health Sciences, Simmons College

----

Korey Hood, PhD, has masterfully written an easy-to-read and engaging guide for teens living with type 1 diabetes. There are many expected pitfalls that confront the growing and developing adolescent with diabetes. This book offers compelling approaches to avoiding these hazards, using dialog that is understandable, humorous, and compassionate. There are no imperatives; rather Dr. Hood provides the teen with realistic choices and opportunities so that diabetes can become a priority AND fit into the unpredictable lifestyle of adolescence. I encourage teens with type 1 diabetes, their families, friends, and healthcare providers to read this book.

Lori Laffel, MD, MPH

Chief, Pediatric, Adolescent, and Young Adult Section, Investigator, Genetics and Epidemiology Section, Joslin Diabetes Center, and Associate Professor of Pediatrics, Harvard Medical School

A Guide to Managing
Your Life With Diabetes

by Korey K. Hood, PhD
illustrated by Bryan Ische

Magination Press
American Psychological Association
Washington, DC

Published by
MAGINATION PRESS
An Educational Publishing Foundation Book
American Psychological Association
750 First Street, NE
Washington, DC 20002

For more information about our books, including a complete catalog, please write to us, call 1-800-374-2721, or visit our website at www.apa.org/pubs/magination.

Book and cover design by Bryan Ische
Printed by Sheridan Books, Ann Arbor, MI

Library of Congress Cataloging-in-Publication Data

Hood, Korey K.
   Type 1 teens : a guide to managing your life with diabetes / by Korey K. Hood ; illustrated by Bryan Ische.
     p. cm.
   ISBN-13: 978-1-4338-0788-6 (pbk. : alk. paper)
   ISBN-10: 1-4338-0788-2 (pbk. : alk. paper) 1. Diabetes in adolescence--Juvenile literature. 2. Teenagers--Health and hygiene--Juvenile literature. I. Ische, Bryan, ill. II. Title. III. Title: Type one teens.
   RJ420.D5H66 2010
   616.4'6200835--dc22

                              2010011063

Mixed Sources
Product group from well-managed forests, controlled sources and recycled wood or fiber
www.fsc.org Cert no. SW-COC-003264
© 1996 Forest Stewardship Council
FSC

10 9 8 7 6 5 4 3 2 1

Contents

Note to Reader

It was the first day of high school. Carter had several questions running through his mind as he walked in. What are my teachers going to be like? Will I have classes with my friends from eighth grade? Why can't the summer be longer? It turns out that his first few months of high school went fairly well—he made friends, he liked his teachers, and importantly, he was getting closer to winter break.

But one day in December he felt bad. He went to the school nurse and while waiting in line to see her, a 10th-grader squeezed by and said, "My blood sugar is 158 and I'm going to lunch." Then he walked out. The nurse nodded her head, said, "Okay, thanks," and then wrote something down in a small notebook. Carter had new questions in his mind—what does a blood sugar of 158 mean? and why did he have to tell the school nurse? What Carter didn't know was that he was going to learn more about blood sugars than he ever wanted to know. Within the next few weeks, Carter was diagnosed with type 1 diabetes.

Is this story similar to your diabetes diagnosis story? Or are you a teen with diabetes who has no memory of getting diagnosed because you were two years old? There hasn't been a time in your life when you can remember *not* having diabetes. Perhaps your diagnosis story involves a visit to the emergency room, a longer-than-expected stay in the hospital, and a reaction to your first insulin injection. Well, your story of how you came to have type 1 diabetes is an important one because it has led you to this point in your life when you are reading a book about taking care of diabetes as a teen. There are many reasons you may be reading this book—you want to read it, your doctor suggested you read it, or someone close to you, like a parent or older sibling, said it was "mandatory" reading. Regardless of the reason, my hope is that you read on and take something important from this book.

The stories, tips, and suggestions in this book come from several experiences I've had in my life. First, I'm a psychologist who works with teens with diabetes and their families. I've worked in hospitals when teens are first diagnosed, in clinics where I see teens every three months when they come in for medical visits, and in diabetes camps. I've learned that each teen's experience with diabetes is unique. I've also learned which things help teens take care of diabetes, and which don't.

Second, I have type 1 diabetes. My story is different from yours, however, because I was diagnosed when I was 25. I was in graduate school working on my PhD when I was diagnosed. Ironically, I was studying diabetes. One day, I went to the university clinic and asked the nurse there to let me check my blood sugar. I suspected my weight loss, constant thirst, and frequent trips to the men's bathroom were due to undiagnosed diabetes and sure enough, the meter read "HI." I knew what that meant instantly. Since then, 10 years have passed and most of the details of seeing the doctor later that day are fuzzy, except for a few things—the pain of getting that first insulin injection in my leg, the thoughts in my head (*I wish this wasn't happening*), and how I was feeling (scared because I didn't know what was going to happen).

But this book isn't about me. And it's not just about the thoughts and feelings this shrink thinks are important to talk and think about. This book's purpose is to help you believe in the following points:

- Diabetes is part of your life, but it doesn't have to run your life.
- You can be an expert at taking care of your diabetes. And…
- It takes work to manage diabetes and your life, but you can do it.

Now, much easier said than done, right? Well, that's why *Type 1 Teens* is here to give you a slew of strategies and tips to take control of your diabetes while you're living your life. You're going to learn three major things in this book so you can do that. Here they are.

- Own your diabetes and make taking care of it a priority in your life.
- Advocate for yourself. And...
- Prevent diabetes burnout.

Own Your Diabetes & Make It a Priority

What things do you own? Perhaps you own a phone, bike, books, clothes, or any number of other things. Do you notice that you take better care of something you own versus something another person owns? You might do this because you've paid for it with money you've earned from a job or you got it as a gift from someone important to you.

Well, you didn't ask for diabetes and you certainly would trade it in if you could. That's why diabetes can be tougher to own. This book will describe ways to accept you have diabetes, ways to feel less embarrassed about it, and ways to make it a part of your life. Plus, you'll learn ways to make taking care of it a priority in your life. When that happens, other things fall in to place and you end up getting a lot more out of life and having more fun.

Advocate for Yourself

It's not quite this basic, but being an advocate for yourself means you do something in order to get something you need. Just for the time being, let's imagine that what you want is to take better care of your diabetes. In this book, you'll learn ways to know what you're talking about, how to ask questions, and how to get the kind of help you need from the people on your diabetes support team (parents, diabetes doctors and nurses, and your friends). These strategies will make you a better advocate and you'll know who and what to ask for.

You'll see that you can get a lot out of being a good advocate for yourself and your diabetes care. You'll get more control over things, feel more independent, and be more responsible. Plus, by being more responsible, the "grown-up" things you want to do—driving, going to concerts, getting a later curfew—will be easier to achieve. All this comes from finding ways to advocate for yourself and showing your support team that you can take care of your diabetes.

Prevent Diabetes Burnout

Diabetes burnout is no fun. It's that feeling of frustration you get when you do the same thing over and over again and it doesn't seem to get you anywhere. Maybe you do exactly what your doctor recommends—checking blood sugars, giving insulin at the right times, and exercising—but you still can't seem to get your A1c down. Well, when that happens, you might say *What's the point?* and stop doing what you need to do to take care of your diabetes. That's why it is so important to prevent diabetes burnout from creeping up.

In this book, you'll learn to do that by paying attention to the diabetes burnout warning signs. You've got to pay attention to the thoughts and feelings you get when you're taking care of your diabetes. Then, you've got to remind yourself that diabetes is not always predictable—it might be those raging hormones wreaking havoc. You'll learn how to hit your own RESET button to start over. Start fresh. We'll talk about how different parts of high school (friends, alcohol and drugs, and romantic relationships) are also related to taking care of your diabetes and preventing burnout. One way or another, you'll have new tools to keep diabetes burnout from creeping up.

Let's Get to It

I've taken up plenty of your time with this introduction and there's a lot to get to in this book. One last message and then you're off. As you read each chapter, think about your experience with diabetes. Ask yourself, does this apply to me? You'll probably find it does. And there are a lot of teens with diabetes out there, who like you, might be struggling to take care of diabetes. You're not alone. Try some of the things in this book and I'm confident your daily experience with diabetes will be better.

Good luck!

Korey Hood

Section One

Diabetes is Yours...
Deal With It

Chapter 1

Get Your Priorities Straight

You have a lot going on right now and *everything* is important: school, sports, your friends, a job, dating, and whatever else you have going on. But diabetes also needs to be on that list of important things. You have one more thing to worry about than other teens. And it can seem overwhelming. Taking care of your diabetes is *more* than a full-time job because the person with a full-time job gets to come home and not think about the job until the next day. Diabetes isn't like that. Diabetes is there all the time. It is part of everything you do. This is not easy to accept (I know), but once you do accept it, you'll feel better and enjoy everything else you do. This chapter will help you figure out how to make your diabetes care a higher priority. And this can be done without taking you away from your friends and other activities you enjoy.

To start, let's see how much of a priority diabetes is for you. Answer the 15 questions on the next page by circling YES or NO.

Priority Check

Before you leave the house, do you check to make sure you have all your diabetes supplies?	YES	NO
Do you check your blood sugar as many times a day as you're supposed to?	YES	NO
If you have to do a shot Saturday morning, do you set an alarm so you won't sleep past the time?	YES	NO
Do you think of questions about your diabetes care before your appointment with the nurse?	YES	NO
When your plans change, do you think about how that will interfere with diabetes care?	YES	NO
When you eat extra food or a snack, do you give yourself extra insulin?	YES	NO
Have you ever gone on a website to learn something about diabetes?	YES	NO
Have you ever used an alarm, maybe on your cell phone, to remind you to check your blood sugar?	YES	NO
Do you know how to set the date and time on your meter?	YES	NO
Have you ever been too embarrassed to ask someone else for help with taking care of your diabetes?	YES	NO
Have you ever skipped an injection because you didn't want someone to see you have diabetes?	YES	NO
Have you nudged a parent to stop talking when they're telling relatives about your diabetes?	YES	NO
Do you skip fun things because you're nervous someone there may say something when you check your blood sugar?	YES	NO
Do you pretend everything is okay even if it isn't?	YES	NO
Have you ever told a parent your blood sugar was lower than it actually was?	YES	NO

Checking Your Priorities

So, once you're finished let's take a look at your answers. If you answered NO more than YES to questions 1 through 9, you're either lazy or disorganized with your diabetes care. This is getting in the way of doing the best you can with your diabetes care. Laziness may keep you from doing your injection on time or doing the extra one you need after a snack. Or maybe you're lazy or disorganized about asking questions during doctor's appointments. We all like to sleep in, especially on weekends, but have you asked your doctor about doing your morning injection later? Being disorganized with your diabetes care may also keep you from doing something spontaneous because you don't have all your supplies with you. All of your friends are going somewhere after school, but you forgot your insulin pen, so you're out of luck. You get to go home. Or maybe you go and just skip your injection. In the next section, we'll see how to do something about laziness and disorganization.

What if you answered YES more than NO to questions 10 through 15? Guess what? This means you're probably embarrassed about diabetes. When you look in the mirror, is it tough to say *I have diabetes*? Or do you skip that extra injection because you don't want someone to see that you're different? Or maybe you know someone else with diabetes, but you're embarrassed that your blood sugars aren't as good as hers, so you don't ask her for help or advice—even when you can use it.

Well, lots of teens are lazy, disorganized, and/or embarrassed. These things get in the way of your diabetes care and can really discourage you from incorporating diabetes more seamlessly into your life. You need to figure out how to work it into your life. That's what we'll do in the rest of the book. For now, we'll go over some basic ways you can start to incorporate your diabetes care into your life and get it on your list of priorities.

Breaking Through Your Barriers

A barrier is something that gets in the way of doing what you need or want to do. Being disorganized or lazy or feeling embarrassed are barriers to taking care of your diabetes. What other barriers are in your life, outside of diabetes? You're nervous to ask someone out on a date—your nervousness is the barrier. You get 25 extra credit points in math class if you look up something online, but you aren't somewhere that has Internet access. That's a barrier. You want to go grab some food with your friends after school, but you don't have any money. Barrier.

So, what do you do about these barriers? Do you come up with a plan to overcome them? The easy thing is to sit by and do nothing. But what happens when you do that? You miss out on something fun or don't do something you have to do. Here are some strategies for overcoming barriers in your life—especially when taking care of your diabetes.

Laziness

It is easy to be lazy. And you may have some good reasons for being lazy— you feel overwhelmed, don't think doing something new will help, or your blood sugars are running so high all the time you don't feel like doing anything because your body is worn out. But you can't sit by and do nothing. In later chapters, we'll go over tips for fixing these reasons, but right now, try the following things to fight the barrier of laziness. Fighting laziness by having fun, taking small steps, and rewarding yourself can help diabetes rise on your list of priorities. And you don't sacrifice your time with friends or in other activities.

Tip 1: Do something fun. It is incredibly hard to be lazy when you are *doing* something. And especially when doing something fun. When you get home from school, pick something fun to do that evening. Pick two things the next night. And make it something other than watching your favorite TV show, talking on the phone, playing a video game, or texting. Walk with your friend and talk about the TV show. And if you love to listen to music, make playlists for everything you can imagine. Go to shows. Get into it. Remember to look at other areas of your life and increase how much fun you're having. It will balance out the "unfun" stuff you have to do for your diabetes.

Tip 2: Start small. If laziness is a barrier for you, you're probably not doing much to take care of your diabetes. If you doctor says to check four times a day and you're checking once, what happens when you think about getting to four times a day? You think *Never gonna happen, doc!* This is why you have to start small. If you're checking once a day, make your goal to check two times a day. Do this for a week. You'll notice that it isn't that bad and you'll be ready to move up to three times a day. The same goes for when you do an injection. Everyone says to do your injection (or bolus) before the meal, but that means you have to take the few minutes before you eat to calculate the carbs. It's just easier to do it after. The problem is that you're not lining up your insulin with what your body is doing with the food. Try doing this once a day to start. Pick an easy meal to try it with—one you're always around for—breakfast, dinner. Practice it over a couple weeks and then see about doing it at a different meal. To beat laziness, you've got to start small.

Tip 3: Reward yourself. You probably don't get many rewards for taking care of your diabetes. It is something you *have* to do, so why should you be rewarded? Well, why not? Yes, it is something you have to do, but you can also work it to get rewards. For example, ask a parent to increase your cell phone minutes for the number of checks you do in a week. If you're usually doing 20 a week and you make it to 30, you could ask for 10 extra minutes or texts. Reward yourself, too. When you've rotated your injection (or pump) sites like your diabetes nurse said, work out a deal with your parents to get out of watching your younger siblings one afternoon so you can join your friends. Rewards are very nice because you get something good and they make you want to do it again the next time.

Disorganization

When you open the cabinet door to your diabetes supplies, do boxes of test strips, old insulin bottles, and broken meters fall out? Do you have your diabetes supplies spread across three rooms of your house, in the car, and in your locker at school? This is disorganization. Like the questions in the quiz, this is a good sign that the biggest barrier to you taking better care of your diabetes is being disorganized. How do you overcome disorganization? You can start by simplifying things. Then, come up with a specific plan that has small parts. Finally, ask for help. Doing these three things will make you more organized, and again you'll see diabetes rise on your list of priorities.

Tip 1: Keep it simple. Taking care of diabetes is complicated. You've got your meter, test strips, lancets, syringes, insulin, and if you're on a pump, you've got extra tubing and insertion devices. You can simplify things by putting tasks together. Maybe put your insulin bottle and syringes with your meter. Or check your blood sugar every time you do an injection. If you change your pump site every three days (like you're supposed to), you could keep the insertion device and pump supplies in a cabinet by the fridge where your insulin is kept. Also, don't be afraid to ask your doctor or nurse to switch the time of your long-acting insulin to something that is more convenient for you—in the evening, the same time you always let your dog out. Put tasks together and simplify things.

Tip 2: Make a specific plan. Making diabetes a higher priority means that you have to have a plan, a plan that is specific and has small parts. When thinking about a goal, don't just say to yourself *I'm going to take better care of my diabetes*. Instead, say *I'm going to take better care of diabetes **when I'm out with friends*** or *I'm going to argue less with my parents **about blood sugars***. Be as specific as you can. Combine this with small steps or changes. *I will check my blood sugar before I go out with friends and when I get home* is a lot better than *I'll check my blood sugar a bunch of times with my friends*. First, it probably won't happen. Second, it isn't specific. Here's another example. What happens when you think about that test that is two weeks away? Do you say *I need to study a lot for that test*? What does "a lot" mean? Be specific. Say to yourself *I need to study 20 minutes each day before I take the test*. Being specific helps you focus on small things, one at a time, that can add up to big changes.

Tip 3: Ask for help. Diabetes is yours and you've got to take care of it. But it sure is nice to have help. You'll feel less overwhelmed and be more organized. Find small ways that others can help. For example, ask a parent to check your blood sugar first thing in the morning, while you're still groggy from last night's few hours of sleep. Put a piece of paper on the fridge and write a note to your parent, like "almost out of test strips" or "need more insulin." They'll know this means they need to call in for more prescriptions. If you don't get much help at home, ask the school nurse if you can stop by her office at the end of the day to do your afternoon injection. Ask your older cousin who lives next door to pick up your test strips because you have to stay home and watch your younger brother and sister. Whatever the case, you've got to ask for help.

Embarrassment

Anything that makes us different can set us up for embarrassment. Most other teens you know don't have to lift their shirt during lunch or at the mall and do an injection. Most other teens don't have to do a check before starting the car to drive somewhere. Most other teens don't have to worry about what others think about them because of diabetes. All of this is true, but it doesn't mean being embarrassed is a good reason for not taking care of your diabetes. It just has to get done. You can start by owning your diabetes. Then, you can reach out to others who understand you and what you're going through. Doing these things will help you battle your embarrassment so you can take control and make your diabetes care rise to the top of your priority list.

Tip 1: Own it. No one in their right mind would keep diabetes if they could get rid of it. That's something we can all agree on. However, if you constantly think about how much of a pain diabetes is and you keep saying to yourself *I wish I didn't have diabetes*, you'll have a tough time taking care of it. Before you can take care of diabetes, you've got to own it. Just like that example from before, can you look in the mirror and say *I have diabetes*? If not, you haven't owned it yet. Believe me, this doesn't mean you have to wear a sign around that says *I HAVE DIABETES*. But you have to admit to yourself that you have diabetes and that it's your responsibility to manage it.

Sometimes we don't own things because we don't understand them. You can own your diabetes by learning more about it. Go to a website like Children With Diabetes and read about what actually happens in the body, how the pancreas works, how insulin breaks down your food, and how people with diabetes are living longer now than ever before. Knowledge is power—the more you understand about diabetes, the more in control you'll feel.

Sometimes we don't own things because we don't like them. Okay, you don't have to like diabetes, but you have to get along. You've probably had to tolerate working on a group project with a classmate you didn't like. You got through it by just doing what you needed to do and moving on. Do that with your diabetes—just do the check before lunch and move on. Don't think about it after it is done. In later chapters, we'll discuss some more ways to battle embarrassment and other negative emotions that happen to teens with diabetes.

Tip 2: Ask for help. This is different from the tip before because you now need to ask your friends for help. Which friend do you trust the most? Does that person know you have diabetes? Let's hope so. Imagine you're out with three friends and another person shows up with two friends from another school. You don't know these other people. You're already getting nervous wondering what the others will think when you do an injection at the table. So, ask a friend to go with you to the bathroom and do the injection there. And if the others ask where you're going, just tell them it is none of their business or say you'll be right back. Over time, with the support of your friends, you may start to feel comfortable doing the injection in front of others you don't know. You can also ask your friends to remind you to check a blood sugar. How much better would it be for your friend to say, "Come on, you know you need to check now," versus a parent saying that? Use your friends to help you feel less embarrassed about having diabetes.

Tip 3: Connect with other teens with diabetes. Go online, go to a diabetes camp, or go to a group meeting about pumps at your diabetes clinic. If you do, you are guaranteed to find other teens with diabetes. Talk to those other teens. Talk about things you like to do, complain about how much your parents nag you, and listen to what they have to say. You'll be surprised at how similar your experiences are. When you connect with other teens who also have diabetes, it will chip away at that embarrassment you feel. And all of your conversations don't have to be about diabetes. In fact, most of them won't be. But you'll find that they understand what you're going through and don't need to talk about it. It feels good to know other teens with diabetes and not feel so different.

Determine Your Goal & Make It Happen

After you try the tips above, taking care of your diabetes will move up on your priority list, which is great. But when it becomes more of a priority, you have a new job. You'll have to identify your goals for diabetes care. I've heard teenagers with diabetes talk about goals, like getting their diabetes in better control so they do better at sports, trying a new way of delivering insulin, learning all the parts of taking care of diabetes before leaving for college, and doing better with diabetes so you don't get nagged as much by your parents. Some teenagers are already doing well, and their parents and diabetes support team agree, so they just want to maintain all the good things going on. Once you've selected the goal for your diabetes care that fits you best, see if you can use the tips above to accomplish it.

Let's take an example. Are you thinking about switching to an insulin pump? You've been doing injections for years and feel like you are ready for the insulin pump, or maybe you're just tired of 4–5 injections a day. If you're already on a pump, maybe you're interested in doing continuous glucose monitoring. What you've read online about it sounds very interesting, but you still have a lot of questions. Now, imagine you met another teen with diabetes during one of your clinic visits. You got his e-mail and cell phone number and now you're talking regularly. This new friend has convinced you that it is a good time to try the insulin pump. He's been doing it for two years. You've been a little lazy in the past about this—it sounds like a lot of work. And you're not exactly the most organized person. And to top it off, you're unsure what others will think when they see the pump. They may say, "Why are you wearing a pager?" or "You can't have that in school." So, what can you do?

Here's one scenario. Start with a **specific goal**—*I will ask my doctor and nurse about going on the pump at my next clinic visit.* Imagine that they say you'll need to check blood sugars a couple more times a day, so you should practice that. You come up with a **small, specific goal**—*I'm going to check at breakfast, lunch, after school, dinner, and before going to bed.* You **ask your parents to help** with reminders, maybe leaving a note on the fridge about the after-school check. You always visit the fridge first thing when you get home from school, so this **keeps it simple**. You also start practicing site insertions, but you've always been a little nervous about that. You decide to practice in your bedroom. You put on some music that usually calms you down. You then do the insertion correctly. No bruising. No bleeding. You keep practicing. You even come up with a **reward** for all this practice and doing more checks a day. It turns out that your parents have noticed and they've extended the amount of time you can spend on the phone each evening. At the same time, you keep **doing something fun** with your new friend. One time while you're hanging out, you also **ask your friend** for insider advice about the pump. You're really interested in what others have asked him about his pump. He gives you a run down and tells you how he usually responds in situations where he could get embarrassed. Within a matter of a few months, you're on the pump and you don't ever want to go back to injections.

Putting It All Together

Just as in the last example, you can accomplish your goal for diabetes care. That teen overcame the barriers of being lazy, disorganized, and feeling embarrassed. All of the tips mentioned so far were used and diabetes care became a higher priority in his life. And doing that didn't take him away from other things he likes to do. In fact, taking better care of diabetes made those areas better.

Throughout the rest of the book, we'll discuss ways to stay on top of your diabetes care. There are more tips, more information, and more reasons to do everything you can to take care of your diabetes. This starts with being an advocate for yourself. Like the teen above, maybe you're really interested in changing a major part of your insulin regimen. Maybe you want to try something new. Maybe you want to switch up your diet and aren't sure if it is a good idea. The next chapter will give you helpful hints on ways to be an advocate for yourself and to get what you want and need. Remember, it is your diabetes and you should have a say in the way it is managed.

Chapter 2

Be Your Best Advocate

How do you get what you want? You do something to get it, right? This is what an advocate does. An advocate decides to do something to get something. For example, a celebrity is an advocate for research on finding a cure for a disease when she does commercials about it. She wants people to do something—make a donation—to get something—money for research on a cure. And you're an advocate for yourself when you convince your parents that you deserve to go to a concert. You do something—tell your parents that you got a good grade on a recent test—to get something—watching your favorite band live.

Well, what about with diabetes? Are you an advocate for your diabetes care? Maybe you've had diabetes for a long time, and recently you've noticed that your doctor and nurse have started asking you what you think during your visits. They are encouraging you to be an advocate for yourself. Or maybe you just got diagnosed and while everything is still new, your parents ask you what you think before any decisions are made about how you take care of diabetes. Are you ready to tell them what you really think?

This chapter will explain why it is so important to be an advocate for your diabetes care and give you some strategies to be the best advocate possible. Let's start with more about why it is so important to be an advocate for yourself.

Why Be an Advocate?

The simplest answer to this question is to get what you want and need. So what do you want from diabetes, outside of getting rid of it? Do you want diabetes to not get in the way of doing things you want to do? Do you want diabetes to be easier to take care of? Do you want diabetes to, in a strange way, actually make you healthier than you are right now? Being an advocate for your diabetes care can make all of those things happen. Here's how that happens:

- Being an advocate puts you in control of your diabetes care—or at least gives you a big say in it.
- Being an advocate helps you prevent diabetes burnout.
- Being an advocate sets you up for independence as you get older and move out on your own.
- And being an advocate helps you keep health as a top priority in your life.

You Take Control

It feels good to have a say in what happens or to have some control over how something turns out. Have you been part of a group in one of your classes where others listened to your ideas about what the group should do for their class project? Feels good to be heard. Have you been part of a sports team and the coach did what you suggested and the team won? Having a say or being in control feels good. Advocates stand up for what they want to end up having more say in what happens.

The opposite doesn't feel so good. Imagine you were out sick when the group decided on the class project and you got assigned the hardest part of the presentation. You didn't have a chance to be an advocate, and with no say in what happens, you got left out and have more work. Maybe you do have a chance to be an advocate, but you think to yourself *Why do I bother saying anything, no one ever listens?* You don't say anything and what gets decided is the thing you didn't want to happen. Without the chance or the willingness to be an advocate, you're going to get left out.

Have you been an advocate for your diabetes care during a conversation with your parents or your doctor? Perhaps you heard about a new way to inject insulin that might not hurt as much as your syringes or may be more convenient. Then maybe you read about it, asked about it, and told your parents and doctor you want to try it. That's great. You were an advocate. You just got more say in what happens to you. You took control.

You Prevent Diabetes Burnout

Diabetes burnout stinks. When you're burned out, you feel frustrated and tired of diabetes, and what you're doing to take care of your diabetes doesn't seem to make things better. Then, because you're burned out, you stop doing as good a job at taking care of your diabetes. You might stop checking blood sugars as much. Maybe you miss an injection or you don't pay as much attention to what you're eating. Wouldn't it be nice to avoid feeling this way? Wouldn't it be nice not to feel burned out? If you advocate for yourself and your diabetes care, you will prevent diabetes burnout. Why? For one, advocating for yourself helps to keep everything in perspective—nothing feels majorly overwhelming if you're in control and on top of things.

You also keep things in perspective by compromising (we'll talk about that soon) and keeping a cool head. When you have a better perspective and feel more in control, you can set more reasonable goals. For example, don't you agree that an unreasonable goal is to love every second of taking care of your diabetes? That's just not going to happen. If you set that goal, you'd start feeling burned out because you can't achieve it. A more reasonable goal is to find ways to make diabetes a part of your life and to make it less of a nuisance. Advocating for yourself and what you want to happen with your diabetes care helps you achieve this goal. Setting a reasonable goal and achieving it will keep diabetes burnout from happening.

You Build Independence

It may make you nervous to think about your life after high school, but it is not that far away. Enjoy all of your experiences between now and then, but get yourself ready for when you have to be more independent. The nice thing about being independent is that it also means you get to make more of your own choices. Start doing that now. You can get yourself ready by being an advocate because you gain independence each time you advocate for yourself. Each time, you are making a statement that you've thought about what you want and know how to get it. Others will notice—like your parents and diabetes team—and they will give you the option to make more choices on your own.

Your Health Becomes a Priority

Aren't you worried about your health? Aren't you worried what you're going to feel like in 20 years? Have you heard these questions from concerned parents, family members, doctors, or nurses? They ask because they want you to think about how the things you are doing right now will affect your health in the future. But do these questions ever make you want to be healthier, to make healthier choices with diabetes and your life? If you're like me, no, they usually don't. You may just do what they say to get them off your back. But the simple fact is that you aren't going to make your health a higher priority unless you want it to be one.

Being an advocate for yourself and having diabetes care higher on your priority list—like the last chapter gave your strategies for—will help you want it. It will help you want to be healthier now and in the future. This happens because you'll have a different idea about diabetes on your mind. It won't be the "diabetes is so annoying" idea. It will be "I can take care of diabetes and it's not so bad." The other nice thing about being an advocate for your diabetes care is that those questions will probably stop. If they know you're being healthy, they won't ask or they'll ask a lot less.

Become an Advocate

There are a lot of positive things that can happen when you advocate for yourself, from having more control to being healthier in the future. And being an advocate for yourself isn't actually that hard. Just follow these three steps and you'll be on your way to becoming an advocate.

1—Know what you're talking about.
2—Know what to say and how to say it.
3—Be ready to compromise.

Know What You're Talking About

Picture this. You are sitting in your social studies class, listening to another student give a presentation on a current event. You read about that event online a couple days earlier. The other student doesn't get any of the facts right and doesn't seem to have a clue what actually happened. The student gives his opinion about what this event means and he's totally wrong. Completely misses the point. What are you thinking? You're probably thinking that he doesn't know what he's talking about and his opinion isn't going to change anything you do. Could he be an advocate for something related to that current event? No, not a chance.

Now imagine that you just moved and you're seeing your new doctor for the first time. She says to you, "Tell me about your diabetes and how you're doing with it." You're able to tell her all about it because you know what you're talking about. You're the expert on *your* diabetes. Is she thinking about you the same way you thought about that student in your class? No, she knows you know what you're talking about. When that happens, she's more likely to listen to you than you were to that clueless student. You've got to know what you're talking about to get people to listen to you.

You're the expert on how diabetes makes you feel—both physically and emotionally. But you see a diabetes doctor and nurse because they are experts on the medical management of diabetes. That's why you need to work together as a team. And when you want to change something with your diabetes, you can read up on the medical management details or ask questions of people that know. Know what you're talking about first. If you're interested in starting on an insulin pump, changing the times of your injections, changing the type of insulin you're on, or checking less frequently during a certain part of the day, talk to your team about it. Ask questions and find answers from people and websites. You've got to know what you're talking about to be an effective advocate.

Know What to Say & How to Say It

Even if you know what you're talking about, saying it the wrong way can hurt you when you're trying to be an advocate for yourself. Has there been a time when you thought to yourself as someone else was talking *If he just didn't seem so arrogant, I'd listen?* We get turned off when people talk down to us or say something in a rude way. Avoid that when you try to get your message across. Below are some examples of how to rephrase your message to make sure you say it the right way.

Scripts for Talking About Diabetes

INSTEAD OF...	SAY...
I'm not checking my blood sugar then!	That's not such a good time for me to check my blood sugar. What's a different option?
I've been sitting in the waiting room **forever**. Can I just get my prescriptions and leave?	It seems like the clinic is backed up and I need to get home by four. Can I just get my prescriptions now and reschedule my appointment?
Why won't you let me start on the pump?	I would like to start on the pump, but it seems like it's taking a long time. What do I need to do to make this happen quicker?
I'm not crazy. Why do I have to see the psychologist?	I don't think anything's wrong, so why do you want me to see the psychologist?

The statements in the *Instead of...* column aren't going to get you what you want. The other statements are much more likely to get you what you want. They are statements good advocates make. Of course, there are countless ways to phrase ideas and just as many situations in which you'll find yourself needing to be an advocate. Try to come up with your own as each situation arises—you can use the examples above as jumping-off points.

But what happens if you know how to say it the right way, but you're too nervous to say it or you're worried you will forget the details? Here are some tips:

- Make notes. Write down exactly what you want to say and take it with you. Don't be embarrassed to look at it as you're talking.
- Practice. Tell someone else what you want to say before you say it for real.
- Ask for support. Ask a parent who goes with you to your appointments to have your back. Tell them what you want them to say to the doctor or nurse that supports what you say.
- Listen first. Before you say what you want, listen. You can be a better listener by making eye contact, re-stating what they said, and nodding your head that you heard them.

- Be nice. No, we're not back in kindergarten, but "be nice" is still important. You are much more likely to get your way if you say something nice.

Here's an example of how all of this could play out. To get your driver's license, you'll have to take a paper or computer driving test and show an instructor that you can actually drive safely and follow traffic laws. You may also be required to do a driver's education class or log a certain number of hours of driving with an adult. Let's assume that you've done everything you need to do to get your driver's license and there is just one thing left—talking to your diabetes doctor so she will sign off on you driving. Most places require a person with a chronic disease—like diabetes—to have a doctor's note prior to getting a driver's license. Are you ready to go in to your doctor's visit and ask for the letter?

Here's one way you could do it. First, you **know what you're talking about** because you've done everything you need to. You're prepared. Second, you **write down what you want to say and practice** it in front of the mirror because you're nervous you'll forget it in the appointment. Third, in the car ride to the doctor's office, you ask your mom to bring it up at the beginning of the appointment just to be sure the doctor knows you want to talk about it. Fourth, in the appointment, you make sure to **be polite and patient** with your doctor. You **listen attentively** as the doctor describes a couple new types of insulins. Finally, you **state your case**. "Thanks for the info on the new insulins. As my mom mentioned, I'd like to get my driver's license. I've done all of the required driving hours and passed all my tests." And then remind your doctor that you're responsible by saying, "I also plan to check my blood sugar prior to getting in my car. Every time I drive." (This is very important. You never want to start driving without knowing what you blood sugar is.) Once you have explained your request, after putting in all the work ahead of time and being an advocate for yourself, your doctor will probably sign the letter and you'll be all set.

Be Ready to Compromise

Good advocates are ready to compromise. They understand that part of getting what you want is being ready to help others get what they want. Being ready to compromise means that you're willing to listen to the other side, you know what you won't compromise on, and you know what the pros and cons of compromising are. Here's an example.

You're annoyed with your parents because it seems like they are making all kinds of decisions for you. Maybe you just made the high school soccer team and during the first practice, you notice your mother talking to the coach. You think to yourself *Why is she here, talking to my coach?* You finish practice and then the coach stops you afterward. He says that your mother told him about your diabetes and that you should check your blood sugar at least three times during every practice. And that the coach will always have some Gatorade around in case you start going low. How do you feel at this point? Aggravated would be a safe bet.

When you get home, you have two options for how to be an advocate for yourself. You could get really angry at your mother for not letting you have the chance to tell your coach and set up a plan. Or you could talk to her in a calm way and advocate for yourself being the person that needs to talk to people like your coach. You may try to say something like, "I know that you were just trying to help, but I'm in high school now and I can tell my coach what the plan is for my diabetes." Maybe you can suggest that next time this comes up, you and your mother will talk about the plan together and make decisions together, but you will be the one who talks to your coach. That's the compromise. Have you been in a situation like that?

There are some basic steps you can follow when you're starting to compromise, and they can apply to almost every situation (including ones that aren't about diabetes). Here they are:

1—Identify the situation. (My parents want me to take more responsibility for my diabetes care.)
2—Know your position. (I don't mind doing parts of my diabetes care, but I still need help with everything else I've got going on.)
3—Understand, or at least identify, the other perspective. (My parents say I should be doing everything for my diabetes care now because I'm 17.)
4—Think of what you're willing to give a little on and what you're going to hold firm on. (I don't mind doing *some* parts of my diabetes care, but I won't do everything. I've got a lot going on.)
5—Meet and negotiate a compromise. (I'll check blood sugars and give myself injections. My parents will e-mail blood sugar results to my doctor and fill prescriptions.)

Sometimes the first round of negotiations don't work, or you think that the compromise is unbalanced, not in your favor. If this happens, go back to the drawing board and review the situation and what you're willing to give on. Then you can talk to the other person (or people) about how you'd like to try for another compromise. But you've got to advocate for yourself.

Putting It All Together

Being an advocate for yourself opens the door for good things to happen to you. The simplest thing is getting what you need and want. It can be about diabetes or something else in your life. Being an advocate also gives you more say in what happens to you, a better chance at gaining independence, and being healthier. Good advocates do three things. They know what they're talking about, they know how to say it, and they are always ready to compromise. Doing those things and becoming an advocate for your diabetes care also does one other thing—it helps to prevent diabetes burnout. That's the focus of the next chapter.

Chapter 3

Fight Diabetes Burnout

I do everything right but it doesn't get me anywhere. When was the last time you thought that? The last time you felt burned out? Like the time you were studying vocabulary words over and over, but couldn't learn them. You looked at the word, then looked at its definition, then said it out loud. Then you put away the definitions and took a practice test and did miserably. You said *I'll never learn these words* and gave up. Or the time you had that part-time job and did the same thing every day. You got there, did your job, left after four hours, and then you were back again the next day. That got old. You got sick of the job and stopped trying. Then, your already irritable boss reminded you that you needed to work harder. That only made it worse.

What about with diabetes—ever feel burned out? You check your blood sugars like your doctor said, but it doesn't get you that A1c you were hoping for and doesn't get your parents off your back. It doesn't make diabetes less of a pain. Diabetes burnout is the feeling you get when you do the same thing over and over again to take care of your diabetes, but you feel like it is not helping or getting you anywhere. You feel frustrated, annoyed, and disappointed. And then you stop doing what you're supposed to do to take care of your diabetes. Everyone with diabetes has been there at one point or another. It may have happened to you recently.

Wouldn't it be nice if there were things you could do to fight off burn-out, even before it starts? Well, there are:

- Notice the warning signs of diabetes burnout.
- Remind yourself that diabetes can be unpredictable.
- Hit your RESET button.
- Ask for help.
- Control what you can.
- Be self-aware.
- Slow you reaction time.
- Talk to yourself.

Let's get started by taking a closer look at the warning signs of diabetes burnout, how it feels, and how it happens. Then we'll get to the other things on this list.

Notice the Warning Signs

To start, let's see if you're getting burned out. The easiest way to figure out if you're getting burned out is to check for warning signs, like those contained in the box on the next page. Answer each question with a YES or NO.

If you answered YES to any questions, you're probably starting to get burned out about diabetes. Warning signs that are negative thoughts or feelings are part of questions 2, 4, 6, 9, 10, and 11. If you're getting burned out by these thoughts or feelings, you'll probably want to pay attention to:

- Your emotions
- Feeling different
- Anxieties over possible complications

Warning signs that are actions are part of questions 1, 3, 5, 7, and 8. You've given up on switching something about your diabetes care. You've stopped checking as much because you just don't want the information. If you have action warning signs, you'll need to take a look at:

- Your routine
- The unpredictability of diabetes

Diabetes Burnout Warning Signs

----

1. Does your routine feel like it is getting old?   YES   NO

2. Are you constantly thinking about how frustrating diabetes is?   YES   NO

3. Do you check less often than you should because you don't want to see a high number?   YES   NO

4. Do you feel isolated, like no one else can understand how hard it is to manage diabetes?   YES   NO

5. Have you skipped an injection because you felt like it wouldn't matter and it was just too much work to do another injection?   YES   NO

6. Are you worried about what might happen to your body as you get older?   YES   NO

7. Have you stopped going online to chat with friends about diabetes because you feel like it doesn't really help?   YES   NO

8. Did you give up on your idea of doing the insulin pump or trying something new?   YES   NO

9. Do you feel overwhelmed by diabetes?   YES   NO

10. Do you second-guess why you checked your blood sugar in that crowd because you noticed someone was watching you?   YES   NO

11. Do you think that life is unfair because you have diabetes?   YES   NO

Paying attention to these warning signs and understanding what makes you burned out will arm you in the battle against burnout.

What Makes You Burned Out

Picture this. You get home from school on a Tuesday and go to the kitchen to get a snack, like usual. You check your blood sugar before the snack and it is 150. You're happy with that number. Then you total up the carbs from the sandwich and pack of crackers you're going to eat. You do the calculation in your head, like usual, with your insulin to carb ratio and give yourself the right amount of insulin. You eat your snack as you listen to some music.

Three hours pass and it is time for dinner. You stop by the kitchen table where your meter is and check your blood sugar, not expecting anything other than a normal blood sugar. You check and the meter reads 320. You look again to make sure it actually read what you thought it did—320. Now, what thoughts and feelings might be running through your head at this point? Any of these?

frustration   *disappointment*   *anger*

"What?!"   *irritation*   *"Are you kidding me?!"*

surprise   *hopelessness*

You feel like you did everything, like you always do—day in and day out—right and things still didn't work out. And this can happen a lot with diabetes and in life. The really frustrating thing is that the reason it happens in diabetes is not always clear. And this is just one way diabetes can burn you out. Let's quickly go over other ways diabetes can make you feel burned out.

Unpredictability of Diabetes

We like things to be predictable. We want our friends to laugh when we tell a funny joke. We want the math teacher who never gives homework over the weekend to keep that policy this Friday. Diabetes is no different—we want it to be predictable.

Unfortunately, diabetes doesn't always cooperate. Blood sugars aren't always predictable—like the 320 blood sugar when you did everything right. It could be higher than predicted because of something else going on—some insulin leaked out, your body is "hormonal" due to puberty, you actually need more insulin after school than other times of the day. And then it might change in a couple months. As much as we want it to be, there is no perfect way to take care of diabetes. You've just got to do your best. Most times it will work out, but when it doesn't, you're surprised, frustrated, and annoyed. This makes you feel burned out—*I keep doing what I'm supposed to, but I only get more frustrated.* When this happens, you figure it's not worth the effort and stop trying. Unpredictability can lead to burnout.

Same Old Routine

Blood sugar checks, injections, constant carb counting, doctor's appointments. Do you get tired of the same old thing? Probably. As much as you want the outcome of your diabetes care to be predictable, having the same routine, day in and day out, gets boring. And when it does, it can make you feel frustrated, annoyed, and tired. In other words, burned out.

Feeling burned out can also start with thoughts about diabetes. It takes a lot of mental energy to take care of diabetes. Thoughts about how many carbs are in your food, how much insulin that means you need, what you should do at a certain blood sugar, and where you're going to find a sugary drink if you're going low. With this much on your mind, you can get burned out. Both the things you do and things you think about with your diabetes care can make you feel burned out.

Feeling Different

Are you ever embarrassed to check a blood sugar in front of someone else? Like we discussed in the first chapter, being embarrassed can push diabetes down on your priority list. It can also make you feel burned out. That happens because doing that certain thing for your diabetes—like a blood sugar check—can make you feel different from others.

Are there other things in your life that make you feel different from others? Perhaps it's the music you like that no one else listens to or your choices of electives in high school. You like the artsy classes that none of your friends take. These things, just like being the only one with diabetes, can make you second-guess yourself sometimes. *Maybe I shouldn't have taken that class. Now everyone gives me crap.* Or you second-guess just how comfortable you feel doing an injection in the middle of a crowd. This wears on you. As you get worn down by constantly second-guessing yourself or feeling embarrassed, you get burned out. You stop doing those things. Diabetes care can go down the drain.

Worried About Complications

Complications describe any bad thing that can happen to your body because of diabetes. Usually, your diabetes team talks about complications to your eyes, kidneys, or the nerves in your body. There's nothing fun about thinking about complications, but you've probably been told that keeping your blood sugars in a tight range should delay when complications start or avoid them altogether. The Diabetes Control and Complications Trial (DCCT) study in the 1980s and 90s taught us that. Basically, they found that keeping blood sugars lower and in a tight range will help to lower your A1c. When your A1c is lower, you are less likely to develop complications.

Are you worried about getting complications? A lot of worry can make things worse. If you worry too much about complications, you might stop doing the things that remind you of complications. Things like checking your blood sugar. When it reads 350, you think that means you're definitely going to have problems with your eyes. You think *It is better not to know that I'm high*. Worry is another one of those things that takes up mental energy and puts you on the verge of diabetes burnout. The next section talks about other emotions that can cause diabetes burnout. The tough part is that these are normal emotions—ones that every teenager faces on a daily basis. Soon, we'll tackle strategies for lowering how much worry you have and dealing with this emotional rollercoaster of adolescence.

Emotional Rollercoaster

Do your days ever feel like you are riding an emotional rollercoaster? You wake up and notice it's nice outside. You're happy. You get downstairs and notice there's nothing for breakfast. Now you're irritated. It gets worse when your ride to school is late and you have to stop in the office to get a late pass. More irritated. Then, after your first class, a friend stops you in the hall and tells you about a party he's having over the weekend. Excited. Your boyfriend (or girlfriend) ignores you to hang out with some friends. Hurt. This goes on the entire day—you experience different feelings and all for different reasons.

Now, the problem is that the stress of constantly changing emotions can leave you feeling overwhelmed. You might even feel unsure of yourself because things seem to be changing so much. Well, every teen goes through this. It's partly because teens are changing socially and getting interested in other things. And partly because hormones are raging and that can affect your emotions (we'll talk more about this later in the book). One big issue for you, because you have diabetes, is that these emotional ups and downs can really affect how you feel about your diabetes. When you're feeling overwhelmed about all the non-diabetes things in your life, you probably won't even want to deal with your diabetes. And maybe you're not paying as close attention to your diabetes, so when you do check, you get frustrated at high blood sugars or start worrying about your health. All of this can lead to diabetes burnout. So it's important to use some of the same strategies (we'll get to them really soon) to battle diabetes burnout to also battle feeling overwhelmed by the emotional rollercoaster. Sometimes you might need to take a break from the emotional rollercoaster, or at least not ride in the front seat with your arms raised the whole time. Let's see how that's possible.

Steps to Fight Diabetes Burnout

Let's go back to that blood sugar of 320. Imagine that the loudest thought in your head after seeing that number is *Are you kidding me?! There's no way that's right!* and you shove the meter in a drawer, walk away, and stop checking blood sugars the rest of the evening. Not so wise, but perfectly understandable. But what would happen if you realized that you didn't consider the serving size on the crackers wrapper and actually gave yourself less insulin than you needed? If that happened, you may instead be thinking *Oh, that's annoying, but I gotta remember that the next time I eat those crackers.* You may feel less frustrated and just go ahead and include a correction dose of insulin when you give yourself insulin for dinner. Now, the second ending to the story of the 320 blood sugar is the one we want—you corrected with insulin and while you may be a little annoyed, you don't end up doing anything that may be problematic. You just move on. Here's how we do that and battle diabetes burnout:

- Step 1: Acknowledge the burnout
- Step 2: Remind yourself that diabetes can be unpredictable
- Step 3: Push the RESET button

Step 1: Acknowledge the Burnout

We talked about owning your diabetes in the first chapter, and we'll talk about it some more throughout the book. What's so important about owning your diabetes? Well, once you own something (accept it), you can then start working on making it better. That's exactly the same deal here. Once you notice the warning signs, say to yourself *Wow, I think I'm burned out.* And then do something about it.

This can happen by trying to connect the dots in your mind. For example, you keep thinking *What's going on? I just can't seem to stay on top of my diabetes. Plus, I'm so tired of the annoying people at my school constantly creating drama.* Then you're at a doctor's appointment and she asks you why you're only checking once a day when you usually check at least three times a day. You hadn't even noticed that you cut down on your checks. Then it hits you, you've connected the dots—you're feeling really burned out. Diabetes is part of it. The emotional rollercoaster is part of it. And you're just not keeping up with it. Acknowledge the burnout and get ready for the next steps.

Step 2: Remind Yourself That Diabetes Can Be Unpredictable

When you get a high blood sugar and you shouldn't have, do you get mad? Instead of getting angry or frustrated or despondent, remind yourself that diabetes can be unpredictable, that there are some things that are out of your control or you're just not aware of. Come up with a phrase you can use each time the frustrating blood sugar comes up after doing everything right—*Maybe this has to do with something I can't explain, just correct the blood sugar and move on.* Just take care of the business you need to—doing a correction bolus or injection.

Sometimes the unpredictable nature of diabetes teaches us to keep trying until we get closer to having a predictable result. In the meantime, you've got to remind yourself that diabetes can be unpredictable and you just need to take care of what you need to do and move on.

Step 3: Push the RESET Button

Maybe you want to get a real button and push it every time you need to hit RESET. Every time you feel frustrated, disappointed, burned out. That could work, but you might look a little strange carrying a RESET button around. Just imagine pushing a big red button that has RESET written across it.

Do this as the final step in the process of battling diabetes burnout.

- Notice a warning sign.
- Try to convince yourself it is going to be fine because diabetes can be unpredictable at times.
- Hit the RESET button.

Hit the button and start fresh. Put whatever didn't go as planned behind you and give yourself a break. Taking care of diabetes is not going to be perfect so you've got to give yourself some wiggle room when things don't go as planned or you're starting to get burned out.

More Strategies

Those are three steps that will help prevent diabetes burnout or fight it if it is going on. In the next few chapters, several other strategies will be described that can help, too. They are introduced here.

Ask for Help

Are you the type of person who likes to figure things out on your own? Whether it's a math problem from school or jumping right in to the video game instead of reading the instruction manual that offers helpful hints, you like to do it yourself. Or are you the type of person who doesn't stray too far from your friends or family? You don't need their help all the time, but you like having it. You ask someone to show you how to play a new video game instead of diving in to it yourself. And when that math problem gets a little tricky, you ask the teacher to explain after class. Both types have advantages and disadvantages. Some examples are on the next page.

- -

Hopefully from these examples, you can see that having a certain amount of help is the best strategy—not too little and not too much. Balance is the key.

Ask others for help with diabetes and take it. If your doctor or nurse asked you to send them blood sugar numbers because you recently changed your insulin dose, get some help. You could do the checking yourself but have your parent e-mail the numbers to your doctor. This can be helpful because it is one less thing you have to do after increasing how often you check. Having help will keep diabetes burnout in check.

	FLYING SOLO	**GETTING HELP**
ADVANTAGE	Feeling proud after doing something on your own.	Feeling less frustrated going through something because the slower process helped you learn how to do it.
	You learn how to do something **your** way.	You don't feel so alone.
	Someone notices that you took the initiative and you get praised for being creative.	Even if things don't go as planned, you've shared the process with someone else and you can talk (or complain) about it with someone who knows exactly what you're talking about.
	You learn something new about yourself—like your potential to be really good at something.	You have more time for other things because someone on your team did a certain job that's really hard for you and takes a lot of time.
DISADVANTAGE	Getting frustrated after trying something over and over again with no success.	Once you are on your own, you may not know how to do something.
	You don't know if you're doing something right—or you get hurt trying.	You get really annoyed with the person who's helping you.
	You're the only one to blame if things don't turn out the way you want.	Because you're working as a team, it actually takes longer to get something done. You could miss a deadline.

Control What You Can

You might not know it, but you have control over a lot of things. Figuring out what's in your realm of control will keep diabetes high on your priority list, make you a better advocate, and definitely fight diabetes burnout. So what can you control?

- Diet
- Exercise
- Checking blood sugars
- Sleep
- Listening to your medical team

Maybe you don't feel like you can control your A1c. It always seems to be higher than you and others want. You could give up trying to control your A1c or you could get focused on the things that you can control. You could start by exercising a few times a week for 30 minutes each time. You might not notice a change in your A1c for a couple months, but it will help. You have control over that. Also, you might not be able to control what your blood sugar is going to be when you check, but you can control whether or not you check. Each piece of information your doctor or nurse has will help them help you get your A1c lower. And you can control what you eat. See a dietician and get advice about foods that are healthy to eat. You can control that. If you get too far ahead of yourself—like saying *I've got to lower my A1c*—instead of focusing on the things you can control—checking on a daily basis, exercising—you'll have trouble achieving your goals.

Be Self-Aware

You probably noticed that both thoughts and feelings can be warning signs for diabetes burnout. They are both part of fighting diabetes burnout, too. Your thoughts and feelings feed how you approach your diabetes. You've got to know what those thoughts and feelings are—this is being self-aware—to keep your guard up against burnout, to stop it before it really sets in. First, we'll talk about your thoughts.

There are a lot of different thoughts that other teens have about diabetes. Some teens have the image of a needle while others have the image of a blood glucose meter. Others think of the doctor's office or emergency room where they were diagnosed. Or you think of something positive that has happened because of diabetes, like the day when you switched to a pump and felt like you had a lot more freedom. The important point to keep in mind is that your thoughts about diabetes are connected to what you do to take care of your diabetes. It is the thoughts → actions connection. If you are thinking *I'm so tired of having diabetes* or *This is so unfair*, you're probably going to do less to take care of your diabetes. If you're thinking *I can do this and I've got help to make it happen*, you've just set yourself up for success. Be self-aware and notice those thoughts.

Now, what are your feelings about diabetes? It may seem like everybody wants to know about your feelings and you hear that question a lot. Even though there's a chance you have felt annoyed or nagged by this question, it is usually asked because someone genuinely wants to be sure you are feeling okay about your diabetes. They also know that, like your thoughts, how you feel is connected to what you do. It's the feelings → actions connection. Feeling burned out or frustrated or angry or apathetic about diabetes can lead to skipping checks or injections. When you notice these feelings, you're more self-aware.

Slow Your Reaction Time

Whether it is doing a physical exercise in gym class or being the first to answer a question as part of a trivia game, you usually want a quick reaction time. Or when someone sends you a text, you may want to reply with something funny before they put away their phone. But one strategy for fighting diabetes burnout is to do the opposite—slow your emotional reaction time. In other words, slow down how quickly you react with your emotions. For example, don't *immediately* get angry or frustrated when something seems to go wrong. If you are able to slow down how quickly you respond, you will have more time to consider the situation, what your options are, and what might be the best choice for what to do next.

There are a lot of techniques for slowing down your reaction time and giving yourself a chance to think and make an informed, calm decision:

- Count, slowly, 1......2......3.
- Breathe deeply.
- Go somewhere else or step out of the room.
- Sing the chorus of your favorite song in your head.
- Do something physical.

Now, you've got to know when it's cool to use these strategies because you wouldn't want to count out loud during the middle of class after the teacher upsets you. And you wouldn't want to jump up in the middle of hanging out with your friends and start doing jumping jacks. You can count or sing in your head in these situations and you can also excuse yourself. Then give yourself time to come up with an informed, calm reaction to the situation.

Taking several deep breaths can also help. You may want to practice this at home by putting your hands on your stomach and breathing in—if you move your hands out, you know you're taking deep breaths. There's a calming effect to breathing this way in stressful situations. Try practicing all of these strategies over and over again and they will eventually become habits.

Talk to Yourself

Are you thinking to yourself *Yeah right, I need to start talking to myself and make everyone think I'm crazy?* Seems strange, but a way to battle diabetes burnout is to talk to yourself. Just like the phrase you came up with to remind yourself about how diabetes can be unpredictable, you've got to talk to yourself. And talking to yourself can be used to help slow your emotional reaction time. If you have some words (instead of numbers) that help you calm down, you can use those in stressful situations.

Think about this: Do you ever just react to a situation because that is what you've done in the past? You automatically think a certain way every time that situation comes up. Imagine that every Friday you have to take a quiz in your science class. That's the situation. Because you've never done well on those quizzes, as soon as the teacher puts the quiz on your desk, you think *I know I'm going to fail this quiz.* You probably did not tell yourself to say that, it just happened automatically. But if you want to change that thought, you've got to start talking to yourself. You'll stop that thought from happening automatically.

- First, you have to notice that you are in a certain situation.
- Second, talk to yourself in a more helpful way. (How about saying *I haven't done well on these quizzes, but this is a new one and I studied, so maybe I will do well* as soon as the teacher hands out the quiz?)

Take an example from diabetes. You've had a string of high blood sugars during this week. You go to check your blood sugar after one of your parents asked you to and the whole time you are thinking *I know my blood sugar is going to be high*. Again, you didn't tell yourself to think that, it just happened. When it does happen, you're frustrated. This is the start of diabetes burnout. But what if you said to yourself *My blood sugars have been running high this week, so if it is high now, I should check with my parents or nurse to see if there's some reason why*? Or you could just say *Strange week for blood sugars, just do it and then ask Dad to call the doc and figure this out*. Talking to yourself will help fight those automatic thoughts that can start you down the path toward diabetes burnout. Come up with your own go-to things to say to yourself when you hear those automatic negative thoughts.

Depression

Why is depression here? It's here because it is connected to diabetes burnout. Feeling sad or down most of the time may be depression. Not wanting to do the things you usually enjoy doing may be depression. Not sleeping as much or as well as usual may be depression. Depression may also be feeling tired, lazy, or bored. A lot of teens have these symptoms from time to time, but when they're all there or they happen for more than a couple weeks at a time, they should be taken seriously.

For some reason, people with diabetes are at higher risk for depression. Maybe it is because taking care of diabetes wears you down. Maybe there's something going on in your body with hormones. Or maybe it is because you've let diabetes burnout go on for too long. You don't do anything about feeling frustrated and overwhelmed and you end up being depressed. In the next chapter, we'll discuss more about depression and talk about the people who can help you with both diabetes burnout and depression.

Putting It All Together

Diabetes burnout happens to all of us. It may start because you're feeling the grind of doing the same thing every day to take care of your diabetes, or because it is on your mind all the time. It can start when you notice that blood sugars aren't always predictable and the result frustrates you. To fight burnout and to prevent it from happening again, you've got to notice the warning signs. Notice when you're overwhelmed or skipping checks because you don't want to see a high number. Then you've got to remind yourself that diabetes can be unpredictable and just take care of business instead of getting mad at diabetes. Get yourself a RESET button and hit it often. Start fresh. Other ways to battle diabetes burnout include asking for help and focusing only on the things you can control. Work to be self-aware and notice your thoughts and feelings. You have permission to talk to yourself to work on those negative thoughts. Finally, slow things down so you have more time to respond the best way. If you use these strategies, you'll be effective at fighting diabetes burnout. You'll start feeling a lot better. In the next chapter, you'll find out that there are others you can rely on for support and how to get that support. They can also help put these strategies into your daily life.

Section Two

This Is Your Life... on Diabetes

Chapter 4

Coach Your Support Team

So far, you've heard about the importance of making diabetes a higher priority in your life and being a great advocate for yourself and your diabetes care. Both of these things lead to less diabetes burnout. That's definitely a nice thing. But there's another huge piece to keep diabetes burnout from creeping up and that's getting the help you need from everyone on your support team. Think about your diabetes support team as what keeps you going, what keeps you on track. Your support team also helps you feel like you're not alone in your work to manage diabetes and helps you feel like you fit in. If you have a strong support team, you'll be able to trust the members to help when you're overwhelmed. You'll also be able to trust what they say and feel confident in team decisions.

So, just who is on this support team? Well, you're at the center of the team. There wouldn't be a support team without you so you're the most important part. With that comes responsibility. You're responsible for coaching the other members to be sure they are giving you the kind of support you need. You've got two types of members on your team—those on the "essential roster" and those on the "expanded roster".

The essential roster includes your:

- Parents
- Diabetes doctor
- Diabetes nurse and diabetes educator
- Friends

Your expanded roster includes your:

- Friends with diabetes
- Dietician
- Exercise physiologist
- Therapist

There may be other members, too, but these are the ones we will focus on in this chapter. Each member, whether on the essential or expanded roster, has unique characteristics that can provide you with support when taking care of your diabetes. They may do it in different ways—some may help you with owning your diabetes while others may beef up your advocacy skills by teaching you a lot. Some you'll see all the time and others just once in a while. The key part to understand across all the members is that you need their support and you've got to know how to "coach 'em up" to get that support.

Coaching

You're probably familiar with coaches either because you've been on a sports team or watched professional coaches on TV. Effective coaches have different personalities. Some are my-way-or-the-highway type coaches. They run the show and it's done their way or else you find another team. That's probably not the type of coach you need to be for your support team—you'll alienate the members and end up getting less support. Try to be a conscientious coach—you respect the members and their perspectives and you speak to them in a respectful way. Try your best to be assertive in what you want, but not confrontational. We'll talk about some specific strategies for getting the support you need in the right way.

Essential Roster

These are the essential members of your support team for two reasons: they know you better than anybody else and they're the people you'll come in contact with the most about your diabetes. Think about this—some of these members have been there since you were born (parents) while others have been there since you first got diagnosed (diabetes doctor or nurse). So what are the unique characteristics of each of these essential members and what can you do, as their coach, to get the most support from them? Read on and you'll see.

Your Parents

Parents are definitely essential members of your support team. First, well, they're your parents and their job is to take care of you—feed you, clothe you, and raise you. They love you and they want you to be happy and healthy. They also know more about your diabetes than anyone else except you. That's because they live with you, help you, and feel responsible for how you turn out. Second, they are usually trying to find a way to support you and by talking to them, you help them help you.

First of all, your parents cannot read your mind. For them to help you, you need to advocate for yourself and help them help you. The truth is that teenagers can be difficult to figure out. You may be thinking one thing but your face tells a different story. That's why you have to tell your parents what you need from them. Tell them how they can help.

- Start by talking in a calm voice.
- Be as specific as you can. For example, state nicely that you want them to help you take care of your diabetes by sending you a text message reminder after school to check your blood sugar.
- Set some communication "ground rules" that you can all agree on. Maybe you could calmly tell them it would be helpful if they didn't always ask you first thing when you walk in the door what your blood sugar is. You could ask them to ask you something else first.

Telling your parents what you need from them will help them be better members of your support team. But you need to advocate for yourself for your team to work well together. Now, think about the things that you need from them. You depend on them for practical things for your diabetes, like making doctor's appointments and picking up prescriptions, and moral support, by keeping your spirits up when you get really frustrated or finding ways to get you motivated to do something you're a little nervous about. Figure out what you need from them and focus on that.

But what if you can't talk to them? When this happens, find another way to communicate. Finding a different way to communicate with them is temporary and gets around the conflict that happens when you talk. They will always be on your support team (and that's good!), so

- leave notes for them on the kitchen counter. Nice, simple notes making a request ("Please pick up extra test strips, I'm out.").
- use e-mails, text messages, instant messaging. If they don't know how to use them, teach them.
- make a message board in your kitchen, where your family can keep a calendar. Even if you don't talk, you'll still know who's doing what, where and when.

In Chapter 7, we'll go over some more specific ways to get rid of the conflict in your relationship with your parents, if you're having some. For now, these strategies should help to get the kind of support you need from them. Now, it's totally possible that you're reading this and don't have a parent around. If so, think about the person who helps take care of you, gives you a place to live, or seems like a parent to you. Maybe it's your aunt or grandfather or foster parents. The same tips apply no matter who it is you think of as a parent.

Diabetes Doctor

Your diabetes doctor (your endocrinologist) is a really important member of your team, too. Endocrinologists are experts in caring for people with diabetes and know more than anyone else about the best ways to take care of diabetes. So why do you sometimes say *Do I have to see the doctor again?* as you're heading to your clinic appointment? Maybe it's because you haven't figured out how to make this relationship in to something that works for the both of you. Perhaps you feel a little intimidated during your doctor's appointments because your doctor is really smart and you're kind of intimidated by that. Or it seems like your doctor is really busy and you don't want to keep him from seeing all the other patients scheduled that day. But remember this important point: Your diabetes doctor wants to help you be as healthy as you can. She is doing this job because she cares about you and other people with diabetes.

Like with your parents, your doctor can't read your mind, so you need to speak up for yourself and work with your doctor to get what you need so she can give you the best care. Here's how you can do that.

Plan what you want to say. Part of being a better advocate, like Chapter 2 discussed, is finding ways to have more say in your diabetes care. There isn't a better way to do that than planning ahead. If you want to try a new insulin or way of delivering insulin, plan to ask your doctor about it. Look up details online about it and write yourself some notes. It might not end up being a good thing for you, but you won't know if you don't ask. If you need to ask for a note for school or to get your driver's license, write a note to yourself and ask. Knowing what you want and planning to ask about it will make your diabetes doctor a better member of your support team.

Ask for more information. Don't be afraid to ask why your doctor is making a change or ask for more information about the change. Remember, we rarely do things if we disagree with them or don't know why we're doing them. If your doctor wants to put you on an extra injection a day, ask why. If you are told that you need to do an overnight blood sugar check for the next week, ask why. One thing you'll learn about doctors is that they want to be helpful and like to explain things, so ask these questions and you'll quickly learn that they are good teachers.

But what if you still feel like you don't want to bother them with questions and make them late for the next appointment? Well, be prepared and ask a quick question. You'll learn at least some information and you'll probably do better with your diabetes care. This open communication can make doctor a better member of your support team and you a better advocate for yourself.

Make sure it's a good fit. Now, sometimes you just don't fit with a certain doctor. Or maybe your parents don't fit with a certain doctor. For example, maybe you'd prefer a younger doctor or one that is the same sex as you. You think that will help them understand you better. Or you think you'd be better off if your doctor were more direct with you, told you when you're being lazy and how you can do better. You or your parents can ask to meet with a different doctor the next visit and see how it goes. In a nutshell, the more comfortable you are with a doctor, the better you'll communicate and advocate and the better your diabetes care will be.

Diabetes Nurse & Diabetes Educator

Both names are listed here because they go by different titles in different places. This person usually is a nurse and also a certified diabetes educator. You may know this person better than your doctor because you see your nurse more. That's usually the way it works. You also will talk to your nurse if you call in and need prescription refills or have a question. Your diabetes nurse is an essential member because you have diabetes and, like your doctor, your nurse knows the best ways to take care of it. So, the same tips apply here—plan your questions, ask why, and make sure there's a good fit. But there are a couple others that are specific to nurses.

Explain why something isn't working for you. You may feel embarrassed about how infrequently you are checking your blood sugars. You may feel intimidated to explain why to your doctor. Nurses can often be a little easier to talk to (sorry to any doctors reading this). So, if you explain that you have a completely new schedule at school and are totally messed up with your checks, the nurse might be able to work out a new plan with you. Nurses usually have a little more time in their appointments to do this. They also might be the person who talks to someone at your school. Another example is that Saturday morning shot you miss because you want to sleep in. Explain that to your nurse and work together to come up with a new plan.

Ask to ask your doctor. You can also ask your nurse to tell your doctor something that you feel more comfortable saying to the nurse. It could be something about a romantic relationship and your nurse is the same sex as you, so you feel more comfortable saying it to the nurse. The nurse can talk to the doctor and figure out a plan. Your nurse could also slide the letter that needs to be signed across your doctor's desk and it saves time so you don't have to wait until the next doctor's appointment.

Model them being good advocates. You'll soon find out, if you haven't already, that nurses are great advocates for you. Even if they are more direct with you at times, they want to find ways for you to better manage your diabetes. In a sense, they are advocating for you to be a better advocate for yourself. So watch what they do. Notice that they try to come up with specific plans that have small parts to them. Notice that they also consider the other things going on in your life—like sports, clubs, friends—and try to make diabetes management easier and better for you so you enjoy those other things more. Watch what your nurse does and use it as a model to be a better advocate for yourself.

Your Friends

This section is about the final members of your essential roster, your friends. You'll read about different ways to get good support from them and how that support can make you feel like you fit in and like diabetes is something you can manage. Later, in Chapter 6, we'll talk a lot more about friends and how you can rely on them. But before skipping ahead to Chapter 6, think about the following situation.

You're on a class trip and it's the first time for you in this particular city. The chaperons know about your diabetes and maybe even a nurse is on the trip. But it's a different group of teens you're around and you're only friends with a few of them. And they don't know you have diabetes. Because you spend a lot of time doing things away from the chaperons, you *have* to tell someone else that you have diabetes. Why? It's annoying, but it is all about safety. Picture this: You have a low and the other teen doesn't have a clue what's happening. And you're not wearing your medic-alert bracelet, because, let's be honest, it's not the most stylish piece of jewelry you own. The other teen causes a commotion, the ambulance is called, your parents are called, and everyone basically freaks out. Now, wouldn't it have been easier to tell someone in this group of friends that you have diabetes?

This is an extreme example, but hopefully it gets the point across. You have to tell your friends, at least one, that you have diabetes. Here's how that can be easier.

Ask what they know about diabetes. Start the conversation by asking this friend what she knows about diabetes. This will give you important information. If she says something mean about people with diabetes or something completely bizarre, find someone else. Most likely, she will say she knows a little about diabetes. You can say, "Well, I have diabetes. It's not a big deal, but just in case anything comes up, and I don't think it will, but if it does, just tell an adult that's around that I have diabetes." Then move on to something else.

Reassure them that everything is okay. In some ways, your statement will reassure her that everything is going to be okay. But she will get the point even better if everything is okay. You can do that by checking a little more frequently when you're in a situation, like a class trip, that's not your usual activity. Always have a quick-acting, sugary drink or snack in your backpack. Sometimes you don't realize how much of an effect just walking around has on lowering your blood sugar. By telling this other teen some specific information about diabetes and reassuring them everything is going to be okay through your actions, you won't have problems and this teen will be a good member of your support team.

Just talk and hang out. What about when you're back home and around your friends who know you have diabetes, how do you get the support you need from them? Here's another situation where you need to get support from your friends, but this time it is moral support. Imagine you're having a really tough week keeping your blood sugars under control and you feel awful (physically). You decide to ask your friend to come over and hang out instead of going out to eat like you planned. (By the way, you just advocated for yourself.) Maybe you can talk about diabetes, or more likely, just talk about all the other cool things that are going on at school. You're getting some extra support and feel a lot better talking about things. You might start to feel a little less stressed, too, about this past week of ups and downs with your blood sugars. You've just gotten the moral support you need and now your head's a little clearer to figure out why you're feeling overwhelmed by diabetes. You're in the process of preventing diabetes burnout.

Expanded Roster

Now for the expanded roster of your support team. Just because they're not on your essential roster does not make these team members any less important to you. They play a huge part in helping you take care of your diabetes and fighting diabetes burnout. These members usually have more specific roles on your support team because you're usually not around them as much. Here's who they are.

Friends With Diabetes

You can talk to other teenagers with diabetes for a bunch of reasons, but what makes you want to talk to them? They know what you're going through. You don't have to explain it. It's kind of like an unspoken "I feel your pain." Your friends with diabetes also know what it's like to be a teenager. This helps you to feel like you belong, like you fit in. That's very important for your life in general and helping you own your diabetes. So, here are some tips for getting the most out of this relationship and making your friends with diabetes good members of your support team.

Reciprocate support. Even if you can't wait to tell this friend something, listen first. This goes a long way to keep the friendship strong and you may learn something, too. Listen by paying attention as your friend is talking. Look at the person. You can even throw in a comment to show them you're listening. For example, if your friend says, "I had a low the other night that was really annoying," you can come back with, "That stinks. I hate having lows." You're telling your friend that you've been listening and understand the point of the story. And if you listen first, when you need someone to listen to you, your friend will be there. You'll be amazed that when you're feeling a bit overwhelmed by diabetes, they are there to listen to you. By talking about it more, you'll prevent it turning in to diabetes burnout.

Share insider information. From earlier in the chapter, it's clear that your doctors and nurses know tons about taking care of diabetes. But you and your friend with diabetes know tons about taking care of diabetes as a teenager, right now. So share insider information. Tell your friend what parts of diabetes are fine and what parts are annoying. Talking about the annoying parts may lead to a discussion about how to fix it. *I get so annoyed having to take all my supplies from my mom's house to my dad's house.* Your friend might suggest having a set of supplies at each place—one less thing to remember when switching houses for the weekend. You may learn some tricks of the trade for a new part of your body to inject insulin, how to remember to switch your pump site out after three days, and how to keep diabetes in its place and not let it get too annoying.

Dietician

You might have seen a dietician before. They're usually certified diabetes educators, too, but usually not nurses. That's why they have a different category here. And they're on the expanded roster because you'll probably only see them once a year, unless you need them a bit more. Dieticians can help with anything that has to do with food and nutrition. It's normal to think about food a lot because almost everything you do for your diabetes revolves around food. You try to give insulin in a way that matches the amount and type of food you eat. A low blood sugar involves eating or drinking something. A dietician knows what food is good for you and what might happen to blood sugars when you eat certain foods. And how all of that might affect your weight. You may want to talk to a dietician to come up with a plan for meals and snacks that fits what you want and is healthy. When you meet with a dietician, you'll usually sit in her office and talk about what you're currently eating and what you want to change. We'll talk more about concerns about your weight, if you have them, in Chapter 5.

Exercise Physiologist

Have you seen an exercise physiologist? This person is usually not in the diabetes clinic, but someone you'd have to see elsewhere. They know, obviously by their title, a lot about how exercise affects your body. An exercise physiologist with experience in diabetes knows how exercise, the type and amount, will affect blood sugars. Have you had a low while exercising? Have you finished a game, either on a team or just with friends, and were really high? Or have you thought about doing a race, but aren't sure how to handle all the exercise you're going to get and keep blood sugars in a good range? Go see an exercise physiologist to get the answers. They, like dieticians, can give you excellent tips to keep doing the things you want to do, new things you want to try, and to do it in the best way. If you plan ahead and get good advice from an exercise physiologist, you'll feel less frustrated when problems come up with your diabetes related to exercise. This keeps you from getting burned out.

Therapist

Therapists can be psychologists, counselors, or social workers. No matter who they are, if they do therapy, they are therapists. Therapy involves weekly or every-other-week meetings where you talk about feelings, thoughts, and other things. Therapists who work in a diabetes clinic can help you with several different things—accepting your diagnosis or owning your diabetes, advocating for yourself, and preventing diabetes burnout. For example, if you're feeling burned out about diabetes, seeing a therapist can help. The therapist will ask what you're doing to take care of your diabetes, how you get along with those who help you with your diabetes, and how you're doing in school, with friends, and other activities. As a team, you'll come up with new strategies to battle burnout, like those mentioned in the last chapter.

Here are some other common reasons teenagers with diabetes go to therapy.

You're feeling down or depressed. If you're feeling depressed, ask to see a therapist. The therapist will become a good member of your support team by helping you recognize when you're feeling down, why you're feeling down, and some strategies for getting through it. Maybe you always feel down in certain situations because you automatically think a certain way. Your therapist might help you find some ways to challenge those thoughts. You'll hear more about this when we learn some problem-solving strategies in Chapter 7.

You're worrying about your weight. If you're worried about your weight or you're making unauthorized changes to your insulin schedule because of worries about gaining weight, ask to see a therapist. You'll work on why you think about weight so much, and your therapist can work with your dietician, diabetes nurse, and others to come up with the best plan for you. Your therapist will be a good member of your team by helping you directly as well as working with the rest of your team. We'll cover more about this in Chapter 5.

In all of these cases, including the one on diabetes burnout, the therapist's job is to help you find ways to feel better. So, they have to first figure out why you're feeling bad (or feeling depressed or worried). Therapists ask a lot of questions to get this information. It's just like making a change to your diabetes regimen—you're more likely to do it if you know why you're doing it. You're more likely to get better in therapy if the therapist knows why you're feeling bad. Here's how you can help the therapist and help yourself get the most out of your therapy.

Be open and honest. You don't have to come in to a therapy session and reveal everything about yourself, but you have to be open and honest when answering questions. It's okay, this information is not going to get out. The therapist is not going to blog about it on the web. Therapists are not allowed to do that because what you say is kept confidential. And therapists who work with teens a lot will work out an agreement with your parents—with your approval—that says the therapist can tell general things to your parents ("He's feeling down and we will work on that in therapy" instead of "He's feeling down because his girlfriend dumped him, he doesn't have any friends, he hates diabetes, and we need to do lots and lots of therapy to get that fixed"). The therapist's office is a safe place to be open and honest about what's going on in your head. Use that to your advantage to feel better.

Ask tough questions. Just like your diabetes doctor makes changes and you have a right to know why, your therapist sometimes makes suggestions or gives you homework and you should ask why. There's usually a good reason. If they ask you to write down your mood a few times a day and what you're doing at those times, you should ask why. The therapist will say that the first part of feeling better is knowing the times and situations when you're feeling bad. Ask tough questions of your therapist. It's your right and it makes it even—they will ask you plenty of tough questions.

Putting It All Together

Your diabetes support team is made up of who can help you manage your diabetes. You're the coach and there are essential and expanded rosters. This chapter gave you tips for talking to these people and letting them know how you can work together to get you the support you need. When you do this, you're doing all the things we've talked about so far in this book. You're advocating for yourself when you ask questions to understand why a change is being made. You're making diabetes a higher priority when you show up at clinic appointments ready to ask questions and make changes to take better care of your diabetes. And you've prevented diabetes burnout when you decide to talk to a therapist. You want to talk to a therapist to find ways to make diabetes less of a nuisance, generate less frustrating thoughts, and get back on track to doing and feeling better. You might be able to do some of these things on your own, but use your support team and get the most out of them. The next chapter keeps at it by talking about responsibility. You're a teenager now. Are you ready for that responsibility?

Chapter 5

Responsibility, What's That?

This chapter focuses on aspects of life that every teenager is involved in—things like going to school, driving, working part-time, and, of course, having fun. You might think that if these areas can be navigated successfully, taking care of diabetes will be much easier, and for the most part it's true. Well, it goes the other way, too. Look at it this way, if your blood sugar is swinging inconsistently, you can't really focus on your homework, driving, or your job. This chapter will focus on how you can take on the responsibilities that come with getting older and having diabetes, and still have fun with your friends and do everything else you want to do. This seems like it's a lot to cover, so let's focus on the big stuff:

- Making good decisions is part of being responsible
- Getting organized helps you be more responsible
- Doing "grown-up" things makes you look responsible
- Taking care of yourself is the most responsible thing you can do

Making Good Decisions

One key aspect of responsibility is making level-headed decisions. A big part of that is not letting your feelings get in the way of decisions that have to be made. Now, you can't *not* have feelings—that's impossible. But it does mean that you can try to not let them get in the way of making decisions. Feelings can sometimes cause us to make decisions that are not the best for us (Remember Chapter 3 on diabetes burnout?). Another part is having a good plan for solving problems. Just about every decision you make can be thought of a problem you have to solve.

For example, say you've climbed to the top of the high school student government and now you have to pick your "cabinet." You are really interested in government and want to take this seriously. You may even want to study political science when you go to college. You have a few goals—getting more activities for students after school, getting a new TV for the student lounge. Now you're faced with tough decisions about who to pick for each position. You get e-mails and calls from all of your friends. You really like your friends and have a lot of fun with them. You can't think of anything better than hanging out with your friends during "official" time.

Then it hits you. Maybe your friends won't be good at these jobs. You can think of three to four other classmates who could do the job better. You are now faced with going with your feelings—you feel connected to your friends, enjoy their company, and don't want them to be mad at you—or putting those feelings aside and making a good decision. It is a tough decision, but you end up picking the most qualified for the positions, who happen to not be the friends who e-mailed and called you. You were able to put your feelings aside when making important decisions.

This is not as easy as it sounds. Take a look at the box on the next page to see some strategies for making decisions—these all have to do with solving problems.

You can use these five steps for every problem you have to solve:

1—identify
2—brainstorm
3—list pros and cons
4—pick a solution
5—test it

STEPS FOR SOLVING PROBLEMS & MAKING GOOD DECISIONS	EXAMPLES
Identify the problem.	**School.** You have to decide between your friends and other more qualified classmates for "cabinet" positions. **Diabetes**. You have to decide which way to go—your doctor has given you the choice of doing injections or using an insulin pump.
Brainstorm solutions.	**School**. You have three choices: 1) go with you feelings and "hire" your friends, 2) hire the more qualified people, or 3) hire a combination of both. **Diabetes**. You have at least three choices: 1) go with injections, 2) go with the pump, or 3) stick with injections but start reading up on the insulin pump.
List the pros and cons of each solution.	**School**. If you hire both, you'll be around your friends and get some work done (pros). But you won't get as much done as you would if you just hired the qualified (con). **Diabetes**. Injections are annoying and take up time (con), and you know the pump well because other friends use it (pro). But the process to get on a pump takes time (con).
Pick a solution.	**School**. You decide to hire just the qualified people but to let your friends know that you may have a future position for them. **Diabetes**. You decide to try the insulin pump and start the process for getting on it.
Evaluate your selection.	**School**. In two months, your team didn't make much progress. You decide to contact your friends to see if they can help you do better. **Diabetes**. You set up appointments with the dietician, nurse, and therapist to discuss the pump. After that, you will decide whether to move forward now or wait.

You can even use them for every decision you have to make. If you take this approach, you'll make more level-headed decisions that aren't influenced by the feelings you have. You may also want to list your feelings in the pros and cons—*If I do this, I may feel disappointed with myself.* With these five steps in mind, let's review other ways to be more responsible with diabetes and the rest of your busy life.

Getting Organized

Early in the book (Chapter 1), we discussed how disorganization can get in the way of taking care of your diabetes and making that a priority for you. But what does the opposite—being organized—look like? Well, you may be organized if any of the following are true: your locker at school is neat, your room at home is clean, or you have a different folder for every one of your classes and activities. If none of those is true, you may still be organized if your CDs and DVDs are filed alphabetically on your shelves or all your clothes are put away, with pairs of socks matched up. There are lots of other ways to be organized, too, but what are the benefits of being organized?

In general, being organized helps you accomplish your goals and keeps you from feeling stressed. When you know where something is, you spend less time being stressed trying to find it. When you have a list ordering the eight chores you have to get done and check them off when each is done, you stay on track to finishing everything so you can go hang out with your friends. It's the same with diabetes. If you need to check your blood sugar and can't find your meter, you may get stressed or just not check. If you're getting your stuff together for a class trip, like the one mentioned in the last chapter, but you can't find the right clothes, your headphones, or your money, you'll be stressed and probably late. So, it's important to be organized. We'll cover two strategies that can help get you organized and stay that way.

Set Your Priorities

Part of being organized and responsible is setting priorities. Yes, priorities are a big deal, and the older you get, the more things you'll have to prioritize. This was discussed in the first chapter and it is the same idea here—identify the most important aspect of something you want to achieve and then work on that. Imagine this: It's getting close to the end of the grading period at school. You've got exams, a term paper to complete, and it also happens to be your best friend's 16th birthday and her mom asks you to help plan the party. Everything is due in two weeks. One way to help prioritize your activities over those two weeks is to write down a list of things that need to be done in each category. Then rank them from easiest to hardest to get done. Also put a star beside the things that absolutely have to get done, like sending an e-vite to all your friends about the party. To review,

1—write down everything you have to do
2—rank them from easiest to hardest
3—star the have-to-get-done items
4—start with the easiest

If you start with the easiest task, you'll feel like you've accomplished something when that's done. That gives you energy to work on the things you've starred. The things that *have* to get done are usually harder and use up more of your time. When you are getting close to your deadline and you see that there are two starred items left and two non-starred items left, just focus on the starred items. You may even need to add in the five problem-solving steps above if you're struggling to solve a problem during this process.

Now, let's not forget about diabetes during this time. You can do that by including diabetes as a category on your list. Write out what you need to do across those two weeks and be specific. If you keep your blood sugars in good control during that time, you'll be able to focus more on getting the other things done. Have you tried concentrating on something when your blood sugar is 350? It's hard to concentrate when that happens. By setting your priorities in this way, you should be able to accomplish your goals and feel less stressed during the process.

Manage Your Time

Another big component of being organized is using time wisely. How do you use time wisely? Maybe this is an old saying and it doesn't mean anything to you. Basically, the idea is that you don't waste time. Sounds kind of boring, huh? Well, adopting just a few strategies may help you use your time more wisely while still having fun.

Let's start with diabetes. Because you have to do things to take care of it, it adds time to what you have to do during the day. You may feel like this takes time away from other things you *have* to or *want* to do. But is that really the case? Between checking blood sugars, carb counting before meals, giving insulin, and treating lows or highs, you probably spend less than 15 minutes a day doing these diabetes tasks. Don't you agree? What takes up more time is the *thinking* about diabetes. Thinking about what you need to take with you when you leave the house in the morning. Thinking about why your blood sugar was higher than it should've been. Thinking about where you left your meter when you need to check. Thinking about which site to rotate to before an injection (or moving your pump site). Thinking (and waiting) to see if you drank enough juice to bring your blood sugar back up. If you're organized with your diabetes, you'll end up spending much less time thinking about diabetes. You've used your time more wisely and have plenty of time for everything else you want to do. Here's how you can use time wisely, with diabetes and other things.

Focus on what you're doing. How many different things can you do at once? Talk on the phone while IMing on the computer…while watching a TV show and paying attention to the song playing on the radio. We have gotten pretty good at multi-tasking. However, to be really good at a certain thing, you usually have to focus on it and remove the distractions. So, when you are attempting to get something done, turn everything down or off and focus on the one task. For example, when you're carb counting before a meal, don't have your headphones blaring in your ears or try to watch your favorite TV show. Hit the pause button or wait for a commercial and then do the carb counting. If you focus more on it now, you'll spend less time later correcting highs or lows.

The same goes for life in general. If you have a homework assignment that you think will take 20 minutes, text your friends and say, "I'm busy for the next 20 minutes, will text you later." I don't want to suggest turning off your phone—that might never happen. But if you focus on that homework, it will take 20 minutes instead of 40.

Guess how long it will take to get something done. Decide how much time you need to spend on something before starting it. Make an educated guess about how long it will take. Then, schedule your time. You may want to write out an actual schedule. Yes, it may be a little dorky, but it will help. For bigger projects, maybe like that term paper, you may want to set a timeline on a calendar (most computers and phones have calendars if you don't want to use a paper calendar). Start with the date it is due and work back. *Due date is May 25* *for this 8-page report so I have to get 2 pages done each week starting April 25.* Give yourself a reward when you finish each set of two pages.

Take breaks. Seems like taking breaks wouldn't be helpful to using time wisely, but it actually is. There is no reason to work all the time and even if you are under a deadline, take breaks. Make your breaks enjoyable and make them a reward for getting something done. Make the breaks fun, too, by doing something you like to do—listening to music, calling a friend, or just sitting back and relaxing. It'll take your mind off of what you've been doing so you can hang out and recharge.

Doing "Grown-Up" Things

What's so appealing about being an adult? It's the freedom, right? Freedom to make more of your own decisions, freedom to stay out later, freedom to go where you want with your car, and freedom to take care of diabetes the way you want. Of course, there's a catch. The catch is that all of those things require more responsibility. More responsibility to get to that point and more responsibility so you don't mess up all those extra freedoms. If you start now and show you're being more responsible with grown-up things, you'll get there more quickly and have more success when you get there. Here are a few examples of ways to look grown-up and opportunities to show you're being responsible with your diabetes.

Be Extracurricular

Most adults are involved in a lot of different activities—job; going to the gym after work; spending time with friends; hobbies, like fixing up old cars; and being in a romantic relationship. It's probably appealing to you right now, but it does take responsibility to maintain that lifestyle. Start now by getting yourself involved in different activities. The example before involved someone being part of student government, but you can get yourself involved in sports, clubs, volunteering, or doing something important in your community. A key part to being able to do these things is to keep doing a good job taking care of your diabetes. Here are some ideas to start getting involved:

- Plan ahead. If you're staying after school and usually like to have a snack after school, but your insulin stays at home, you're going to need to take it with you. Plan out when you'll do the injection and where you'll do it. And who is going to help you, if you want help.

- Find some way to link up your diabetes with the activity. Maybe you want to volunteer in a medical setting, so why not check with your diabetes clinic to see if you can help out? Or you're really interested in doing something with computers for your job, so volunteer to set up a website where teens can go to chat about diabetes. In both of these examples, you'll get the experience you want while staying focused on your diabetes. And you're likely to be given more independence by your parents and teachers.

What if you're nervous about meeting new people and finding the right extracurricular activity? Try some of the tips covered so far in the book. Here are a few:

- Be prepared. Before you talk to someone, say the head of the club you want to join, plan out what you want to say. And learn about the club and the people in it so you know what you're talking about.
- Talk to a therapist. If you're really worried about getting rejected, then it may be helpful to chat with a trained professional. When you're so nervous about being rejected, you usually end up not doing anything. You avoid those situations because they feel overwhelming. You and your therapist can come up with some strategies for lowering your anxiety and finding a way to be successful when meeting new people. This will likely help not only this situation, but a bunch of situations that come up in the future.

Work Part-Time

Why do most teens want a part-time job? The paycheck. It is great to have a little extra spending money for the things you like to do. Or maybe you need to work to help out your family. One of the key things to consider is that if you are more responsible with your diabetes, you'll be much more successful at your job. Here are a few things to keep in mind when you're considering taking a part-time job.

Come up with a plan with about how to handle your diabetes at work. This most likely involves telling your boss that you have diabetes. Now, you don't have to do this, but it's a good idea. Tell your boss that you usually don't have any problems with diabetes and it doesn't affect your work, but for example, you need to have a quick-acting, sugary drink nearby. Perhaps you're stocking shelves at a local grocery store and you actually get a lot of exercise doing this. It is really important in this case because you may start going low. You've got something to treat the low, but your boss also knows you have diabetes in case some emergency comes up.

Figure out what kind of job you want. Have you thought about getting a job, but aren't sure which one is right for you? This can be tough because teens usually don't have a lot of options for jobs. But you can try to find jobs that match what you want to study in college or the kind of job you want to start right after high school. Talk to people who have done those jobs and ask friends for help finding jobs. Use the connections you have as long as you plan to be responsible in the job.

Don't forget about school. Trying to juggle taking care of your diabetes, doing an after-school job, and keeping up with your homework can be tough. Doing this successfully shows you're being responsible, and it's impressive to your parents and teachers. Stay organized with your schoolwork by keeping up with your calendar of due dates. Write out what you need to get done and adjust it if you're working certain days and times. And it might be helpful to ask a parent for help with planning out your schedule. And don't worry, this doesn't show you're less of a grown-up. Successful adults know when to ask for help.

Drive

You learned in Chapter 2 how to advocate for yourself when you're ready to get your driver's license, but how do you show you're being responsible once you're driving? Again, this involves some parts about diabetes and just general things. With your diabetes, you've got to check your blood sugar before you drive, every time. Most of the dangers of driving with diabetes come from people having low blood sugars when driving. You can take one major step in preventing these driving problems if you check your blood sugar and make sure you're not low or going low. If you are, don't drive. Correct it and wait. And always have a quick-acting, sugary drink or snack, like Skittles, with you.

Now, most of your driving will be around town and usually just short trips. But what if you're going on a long trip—several hours of driving? Well, this adds a few extra things. You still need to check before you drive and have a sugary drink or snack with you, but you also need to plan out when you'll stop. Is your trip going to cover times you usually eat a meal or snack? If so, plan to stop at those times and do what you usually would do with your carb counting and insulin. Don't drive through some fast food place and do your injection (or bolus) while you're driving. Not safe. It goes back to being focused on what you're doing and if you don't pay attention, you may give yourself too much insulin and have a low an hour down the road. This also includes not texting or doing other distracting things while driving. You'll be safer and show you're being responsible if you do these things.

Staying Active & Eating Healthy

You probably hear from parents, teachers, and ads on TV that you need to exercise and eat well to stay healthy. This is especially true when you have diabetes. You can't escape the simple fact that diabetes can take a toll on your body—especially if your blood sugars stay high most of the time. But that doesn't have to happen. Physical activity makes your body use the insulin you're injecting a lot better. Eating a healthy diet helps to keep your blood sugars from fluctuating as much and gives your body what it needs—like vitamins and antioxidants—to fight some of the things that naturally happen because of diabetes. So, while the last chapter talked about meeting with an exercise physiologist and dietician to get advice on these things, this section has tips for things you can do on your own.

Get Your Exercise

Exercise helps your diabetes stay in better control for two main reasons. Like I said above, it helps your body use insulin more efficiently. The other reason is that exercise makes you feel better physically and mentally—stress relief, time to yourself, and endorphin release (it makes you feel happy). There's a lot of research that shows the benefits of exercising on a regular basis for all of these reasons.

When you're thinking about your own personal exercise plan, make sure you don't forget about certain activities that count in your daily total. You should try to get 60 minutes of exercise each day, and this can include things like walking to and from school (if you do that), gym class, walking or jogging around your neighborhood, team sports, and working out at a gym. Here are some tips for getting the most out of your exercise and staying safe:

- Check your blood sugar before and after your work-out (and maybe during if it's a long period of time or really intense exercise).
- If you're low or going low, stop exercising and treat it.
- You may need to eat a snack before or adjust your insulin levels when you're exercising. Get the help of a dietician and/or exercise physiologist, at least when you start.

There's actually a lot of trial-and-error with this, but over time, you'll learn the best ways to incorporate exercise in your life and be healthier and happier.

Eat Well

Of course it's important for everyone to eat well. This usually involves eating the right types of food and doing it in moderation—not too little and not too much. It's tough to eat right though, with all the fast food choices and foods that taste good but aren't good for you. This is why it is so important to see a dietician at least once a year—to renew your plan for meals and snacks and make changes as your food preferences change. But there are a few things you can do on your own.

Alter how and when you give insulin to match what you eat. You've probably noticed that certain foods make it hard to keep your blood sugars in control. Maybe you were recently diagnosed and you used to eat pizza twice a week—once at home and once with friends. Now, every time you eat pizza and give yourself insulin for it right when you start eating, you feel low about 45 minutes later and then end up really high three hours later. This could be because of how much fat there is in the pizza and your body digests everything slower. So, you may have to adjust how and when you give insulin to match that. With these foods that are tough to figure out, make sure you get help—from a dietician or reading about it online—and be patient. You'll have to practice a little while before you figure it out.

Try to do things in moderation. If you want to eat sweets, try to plan it in to your meals. Maybe your family always sits down for dinner one night a weekend and you always have a dessert. Plan accordingly with your insulin. Or if you're going to have these high-sugar snacks at unexpected times (like a surprise party you didn't know about), have a good plan in place that you've practiced and can implement quickly. You shouldn't avoid these things, but by planning and doing them in moderation, they won't cause you as many problems with your blood sugars.

Watch yourself. Because there's so much focus on eating when you have diabetes, you can start to think about, almost obsess about, food. Maybe you find yourself a little worried about gaining weight or you have gained weight and want to lose some of it. There are healthy ways to do this, and unhealthy ways. The healthy ways include talking to your diabetes team about it. Maybe you need some adjustments in insulin or your meal plan. You might also figure out that exercising a little more helps with your weight. But an unhealthy way to control your weight is to over-exercise. If you're exercising 1–2 hours a day or more and constantly thinking about how all this exercise helps you lose weight and hopefully look better, it's time to talk with someone on your diabetes team about this.

Another unhealthy way to deal with your weight or worries about it is by using your insulin to control your weight. They call this "diabuli-mia" and it involves keeping your blood sugars just high enough so that they burn some fat (and thus lose weight), but not too high so that you end up in the hospital. People who do this use their insulin to try to keep this delicate balance of blood sugars and weight loss. This is extremely dangerous. If you're doing this, you should reach out to someone on your diabetes team, like a parent, or someone else you trust and find a way to get some help. You can also read more about it by searching that term on the Internet. The goal of eating well is to be healthy. If you're doing some of these unhealthy things to control your weight or lose weight, it's best to get some help.

Putting It All Together

This chapter covered a lot of information. Seems appropriate for a chapter on responsibility, huh? Hopefully you get the main message of the chapter—by being responsible with your diabetes, you'll be in great shape to be successful and enjoy all the other parts of your life. Being responsible with your diabetes (and other things) includes having a plan to solve problems and make level-headed decisions. It also includes showing others that you are responsible by doing grown-up things, and doing them well. Finally, it includes a responsibility to yourself by exercising and eating well. The next chapter dives in to relationships with your friends and other teenagers. The main point is to figure out ways to get through the challenges of having diabetes and having friends so that you can enjoy all the great things that come with being around other teens.

Chapter 6

My (So-Called) Friends

Do you spend more time with friends and other teens than your own family? And when you're at home, are you talking to, e-mailing, or texting your friends? It's normal for teens with and without diabetes to spend the biggest chunk of the day around other teens or staying in contact with them. But what are the special challenges because you have diabetes? Take a look at the following statements. These are all things I have heard other teenagers with diabetes say. Any of these sound familiar?

I keep my diabetes a secret until I know someone well.

Sometimes I get nervous meeting new people.

I sometimes get irritated with all the questions about diabetes.

It's annoying when other teens stare at me when I'm doing an insulin injection.

I wish I had some friends who also had diabetes.

I have skipped an injection while out with friends because it wasn't convenient to do it.

I don't feel like going to that party because it will be too much of a hassle.

I have skipped an injection while out with friends because I didn't want anyone to stare.

Now, take a look at the following statements. These are just general statements about what it is like to have friends and to be around other teenagers.

> I don't know what I'd do without a friend to talk to when something's up.
>
> I need to call someone else in my class to find out how to do the homework.
>
> I had so much fun last night at the movies with my friends.
>
> Wait, what movie did we see?
>
> It was great watching the football game with you guys.
>
> I'll get there at the same time as everybody else so I know people.
>
> It's nice to know that someone else gets me.

The point of having you read good things about having friends right after thinking about different challenges of having diabetes is this: We cannot sacrifice the good things because there are challenges. We have to figure out ways to get through the challenges. As a teen (and an adult), you'll make great friends who will be there for fun and support. And you'll meet jerks and idiots who are just plain mean or clueless about you and your diabetes. This chapter is focused on exactly that—friends and not-friends. We'll talk about:

- Your diabetes personality
- Talking about your diabetes
- Feeling different and fitting in
- Being smart socially

Your Diabetes Personality

You may be the type of person who already has a lot of friends and feels very comfortable talking to them and other teens about having diabetes. Maybe you have always been like that or you just recently felt much more comfortable doing that. Or you have a lot of friends but don't talk much about diabetes. Your friends know that if you want to talk about it, you will start the conversation. Or you may be struggling a bit to make friends and you think diabetes may be one of the reasons for it being so tough. Maybe you were recently diagnosed and just now transitioning to a new high school. Or maybe you've lived in one place your entire life and everyone knew you and knew you had diabetes. But now you have moved to a new town and don't know anyone. You say to yourself *I guess I have to tell everyone about my diabetes now.*

These descriptions illustrate that teens with diabetes have different levels of comfort when talking about diabetes. You can call these diabetes personalities. Let's figure out your diabetes personality by completing the box on the next page.

- -

If you mostly circled NOT, you're diabetes personality is to keep it to yourself. You don't like talking about diabetes. Let's put you in the *Uncomfortable* diabetes personality category for the time being. If you circled a lot of SOMEWHAT answers, you're in the middle. You're reserved about talking about diabetes, but will do it if you have to. You're in the *Middle* diabetes personality category. If you mostly circled VERY, you'll talk about diabetes in just about every situation. You're in the *Open Book* diabetes personality category.

So why does this matter? Well, you've got to at least be in the *Middle*, so it's best if you work toward being more open about your diabetes. If you're open about your diabetes, it means you've owned it. You can be a better advocate, keep it as a high priority, and prevent diabetes burnout. So, if you're in the *Uncomfortable* category, we'll figure out some ways to get you to the middle. If you're in the *Middle*, that's great and we'll move you toward the *Open Book* personality.

Let's take a look at two major situations where this is relevant—meeting new people and telling old friends about diabetes.

Meeting New People

Think about the situations where you're meeting new teens. Perhaps you don't want to talk about diabetes in these situations because you're worried someone will think you're weird because of diabetes. Or you're worried that

Find Your Diabetes Personality

For each situation below, think about how comfortable you are. Circle **Not** (comfortable), **Somewhat** (comfortable), or **Very** (comfortable) to determine your level of comfort.

SITUATION	LEVEL OF COMFORT		
Talking about diabetes right after you meet another teenager	NOT	SOMEWHAT	VERY
Doing an insulin injection in front of friends	NOT	SOMEWHAT	VERY
Checking your blood sugar in front of friends	NOT	SOMEWHAT	VERY
You have a low blood sugar at school and another teenager asks what happened	NOT	SOMEWHAT	VERY
In your health class, the teacher says something completely wrong about diabetes	NOT	SOMEWHAT	VERY
Telling a friend at school he's annoying when he keeps asking for information about diabetes	NOT	SOMEWHAT	VERY
Meeting another teenager with diabetes and your parent says, "You'll have a lot to talk about because of diabetes"	NOT	SOMEWHAT	VERY
Pulling out your quick-acting sugary snack in the middle of class	NOT	SOMEWHAT	VERY
Going to diabetes camp	NOT	SOMEWHAT	VERY
Staying in a diabetes camp cabin with other teens (with diabetes) you don't know	NOT	SOMEWHAT	VERY

they've already got incorrect notions of people with diabetes and they'll think you did something to cause your diabetes. Or you just flat-out think someone won't like you because of diabetes. Or you're just shy. All of these things are understandable, and you wouldn't be the first person to think this way.

So, let's start by assuming that the other teen you're meeting isn't going to think negatively of you because of your diabetes. This is actually the case most of the time, so it's not that far-fetched of an assumption. We'll deal with the teens who do think negatively of you because of diabetes later in the chapter. For now, here are two steps for meeting new teens and talking about your diabetes.

Step 1: Decide what you want to say when asked specific questions. No matter what type of diabetes personality you have, deciding how you want to answer questions about diabetes will help you feel more comfortable around other teens. This is especially important when meeting new teens. The last chapter talked about the essential and the expanded rosters that make up your support team. If you're in the *Uncomfortable* category, it may be that you only feel comfortable talking to the essential roster about your diabetes—school nurses, parents, doctors and nurses at medical visits. What do you do in those situations? You probably give just enough information when asked a question. You can do the same when meeting new people, no matter your diabetes personality. Give short answers. If someone asks, "So, why do you have to give yourself all those insulin injections?" you can answer simply, "Because my body doesn't make insulin" or "I have diabetes and that's what I gotta do." Then if they ask follow-up questions, you can give longer answers—maybe about how long you've had diabetes and that you give yourself insulin and check your blood sugar, but mostly, you're a pretty normal teen. Start with shorter answers and only give longer ones when you start feeling more comfortable around the other person.

But what if you're meeting another teen for the first time and you *have* to tell them about diabetes? This could be the case if you're on a class trip (like the last chapter described) or at a summer camp and bunking with someone you don't know. If you've planned out what you want to say, it will be a lot easier. Keep it short, too, until they ask for more information.

Step 2: Practice, practice, practice. Doing something over and over again makes it a habit. And when things are habits, they usually keep you from spending so much time thinking about it. (Remember, it's the *thinking* about diabetes that can take up so much time.) If you're in the

Uncomfortable camp, talking about you're diabetes off the cuff can make you pretty nervous. Once you've planned out what you want to say in certain situations, like meeting new teens, practice it. You may want to practice it in front of the mirror or just repeat it in your head before meeting someone new. And after you've met someone new and used the same lines each time, it will become easier each time after.

Telling Old Friends

The same tips apply here, too. It's good to plan out what you want to say and practice it. But what is unique about telling old friends about your diabetes? Maybe you just got diagnosed and have a bunch of friends wondering why you missed a week of school while you were in the hospital. Perhaps you're at a new school and for the past six months, you've been keeping your diabetes a secret because you weren't sure how your current friends would react. These are both situations where you need some specific tips for telling your old friends.

If you've just been diagnosed, it is best to just be up front with friends. They are your friends because you enjoy doing the same things, listening to the same music, and hanging out on the weekends. That won't change because of your diabetes. You'll have a few extra things to get used to—and so will they—but the reason you're friends with them will not change. Again, plan and practice what you want to say and then just do it. You may also want to come up with a reassuring statement because they may really be worried about you, especially if they don't know much about diabetes. You can tell them about how people with diabetes are living longer and healthier lives than ever before. Plus, you can think of yourself as a teacher and show them different things about diabetes and how you take care of it. It will make you feel better and ease their anxieties about how you're doing.

If you've been keeping your diabetes to yourself, it's time to talk to your friends. What's likely holding you back is your nervousness that they may think negatively of you because of diabetes or treat you differently. So, investigate it a little further and try a few things.

- You can get yourself prepared to talk to your friends by picking a good time to talk.
- Maybe you want to talk to each friend individually or do it in a group. Figure out what will work best for your group of friends.

- You could even start the conversation in a different way than doing it in person—maybe through an e-mail or text. And then follow up in person.
- If you're the kind of person that likes to make jokes about things, you could include some humor to lighten the mood.

You've got to tell your friends, so just do it and try some of these tips to help you get through it. Once you start talking to a friend, you may find out that she deals with something similar and has to take medications every day and watch what she eats. This might make it easier to tell this friend because you share something similar. This leads to the next part, feeling different and fitting in.

Feeling Different & Fitting In

It doesn't feel good to be rejected. It's nice to have a group of friends where you feel like you fit in, amongst people who accept you for who you are. A lot of teens think about fitting in, and many of you may wish you felt like you fit in better at school, in a club or group outside of school, or just in general. One of the things that gets in the way of feeling like you fit in is something that makes you different. So, what can you do about diabetes, the thing that makes you different from most other teens?

Own your diabetes. First things first—you've got to own it. You'll never *feel* like you fit in if you haven't owned what makes you different. For example, are you considered a certain type of person in your group of friends? Maybe you're the person that everyone calls the smart one because you get good grades. Perhaps you're the one that's always cracking jokes and get the reputation as the funny one. When you're away from those friends, you think to yourself *That's kinda cool to be the funny one.* You've owned it. But those things are a little easier than diabetes. If someone says, "Oh, he's the kid with diabetes" or calls you "the diabetic", you might not be so ready to accept that designation. It could be because you haven't owned it and you just can't find a way to fit in. Now, it's certainly not cool of people to characterize you as the person with diabetes unless you've said that's okay, but let's assume for now that you're okay with that. (We'll deal with the jerks soon.)

Tell people you have diabetes. Use the tips in this chapter and ones you'll learn throughout the book. Second, find a way to fit in with other teens with diabetes. Go to local groups supported by the Juvenile Diabetes Research Foundation (JDRF) or do an online chat on the Children With Diabetes website. Building up how much you fit in with diabetes will make you more ready to fit in with friends or other groups. You may even learn some new strategies from other teens that will help you in the future (like the idea of sharing insider information covered in Chapter 4).

Feel good about how you're taking care of diabetes. If you're proud of how you're doing, don't forget to remind yourself that it's hard work and you're doing a great job. Other people will notice if you're being responsible and taking care of your diabetes. Now, maybe only the adults will say something about it directly to you. Notice how good it feels to hear "That's great that you're doing so well with school and all the other things you're doing while also doing a great job taking care of diabetes." But you can bet that other teens will notice, too. They're just less likely to be overflowing with their words—like "Oh man, you're doing such a great job!" or "Way to go, girl, taking care of yourself!" They might say something, but it might just come from your closest friends. If you try these strategies, you'll end up owning your diabetes and will feel much more like you fit in around other teens.

Jerks & Idiots

Have you heard any of these things from other teens?

Why are you doing an injection? Are you on drugs?

Why aren't you eating cake like the rest of us? Is there something wrong with you?

Didn't you get diabetes 'cause you ate too much? Why didn't you stop eating?

You can't keep up with us in this sport 'cause of your diabetes.

Well, these are all things that ignorant jerks could say to you about your diabetes. So what do you do if someone says something like this? You've basically got two choices—ignore them or set them straight. You have to decide which strategy fits you best. If you decide to ignore them, make sure it is because you feel comfortable about it, not because you're intimidated by them. If you say to yourself *They're idiots. I'm not even going to try to teach them*, then you're doing the right thing by ignoring. On the other hand, if your feelings are hurt by what they say or they keep doing it, you can't ignore it any longer. Then you'll need to set them straight. You can set them straight in a few ways—just tell them the facts and end it there, and invite them to learn about diabetes.

Calmly tell them the facts. Leave it at that. "Nope, I didn't get diabetes because I ate too much. I actually didn't do anything to get diabetes." Or "Diabetes doesn't hold me back from being an excellent track star." And it's really hard to do this, but try not to get confrontational. Try to leave off the "…and I'll beat you in a race any day" when you mention your track-star status.

Invite them to learn more about diabetes. Yes, this may seem like it is opposite of what you should do, but it might be good to try. Invite them to read something online or even invite them to attend some local diabetes event with you, like a walk, meeting, or expo about diabetes supplies. This obviously may not work if you genuinely don't like the person, but you may actually keep them from being so short-sighted and ignorant with other kids with diabetes (or any other kind of difference for that matter) if you teach them.

Being Smart Socially

Now for a big part of being a social teenager—being smart socially. A lot of the tips so far will apply here, too, because they all can help in social situations, but what are some specific things to pay attention to regarding your diabetes? And why is that important? Well, as you get older, you'll spend more and more time in social situations. This can be staying later after school to do something or just hanging out each evening with your friends. You can't let your social life get in the way of taking care of your diabetes. Plus, like everything else in this chapter and the last one, by making sure you're doing what you can for your diabetes, your social situations will be much better and more fun. So, here's how you can be smart socially.

Control the situation. To the extent that you can, try to control the social situations you're in. For example, if your friends are trying to find a place to grab some food and then go to a movie, suggest a place you know well. Recommend a place you've eaten at before and you know it will be easy to either slip out to the bathroom to do your injection or do it at the table. You may also be more comfortable with the menu and have a good idea of what you can get and the amount of insulin you'll need to take. If you're able to make the social situation a little more predictable, you'll have less to worry about when you get there and can focus on having fun.

Get help when you need it. This keeps coming up. Remember in Chapter 1 when you were asked to imagine being out with three friends and another person shows up with two friends from another school? You're in a new situation where you don't know everyone so well. You may want to ask a close friend to go to the bathroom with you or to cover for you while you're doing your injection or checking your blood sugar. It is definitely better to be open about your diabetes, but you just may not feel like describing everything to these new people. That's totally fine and you can have a friend help you make the situation a little easier.

Putting It All Together

What type of diabetes personality do you have? If you're not very comfortable taking care of your diabetes in front of friends, other teens, or just generally in social situations, the tips in this chapter should help to move you along. It's important to move you toward being more open about your diabetes because if you don't, you'll continue to feel like diabetes is a burden and you won't get as much out of the important friendships you have. Like the start of the chapter said, you've got to get through the challenges of having diabetes so you can have fun and get the most out of your friendships.

This chapter gave you strategies for meeting new people and telling old friends about diabetes. It also included suggestions for making you feel like you fit in, especially about diabetes. We also covered some ways you can deal with ignorant jerks. In the next chapter, we'll talk about working with your family as a team to manage your diabetes. However, we'll start with identifying the things that can lead to conflict in your family and how you can deal with that.

Chapter 7

Family
Focus

It's your diabetes and owning it, making it a priority, and being an advocate for yourself will make you healthier and keep diabetes burnout from
creeping up. But you're also part of a family, and your diabetes *affects* and
is *affected by* people in your family. Your diabetes affects what your parents
do. Perhaps your mother takes you to doctor's visits, fills your prescriptions, and reminds you when to check your blood sugar and take insulin.
Your diabetes can also be affected by your parents if they aren't involved
enough or you're always arguing with them about diabetes. These things
can cause you to take worse care of your diabetes.

It can be about your siblings, too. Maybe you have an older sister who
looks out for you, like making sure none of her senior classmates pick on you.
But she also looks out for your diabetes by making sure you check your blood
sugar after school. After all, she drives your not-old-enough-to-drive-yet self
to and from school. Do you see how your diabetes affects and is affected by
people in your family? That's what this entire chapter is about.

Also included are strategies for getting the kind of support you need
from your family (like Chapter 4 described). Plus, if you need tips on
keeping conflict in your family to a minimum, they're in here, too. You're
probably going to argue, but by learning better ways to communicate and

get along, you're not going to argue as much. And all that arguing won't lead to diabetes burnout like it might have other times. Let's start first with a little more about *your* diabetes.

It's Your Diabetes

It's my diabetes and I'll take care of it. Have you ever said this to a parent? Maybe you were feeling a little nagged, or perhaps your father was in a doctor's appointment with you and he was complaining to the doctor, "He doesn't take enough responsibility for his diabetes." You felt irritated and this drove you to say, "It's my diabetes" and "Everyone else needs to mind their own business." So, let's examine this a little further.

The absolutely true fact is that diabetes is yours. You are the one who has to live with it. Your body is the body that needs insulin. And your body's response to insulin, eating, and exercise will either make you feel healthy or, at times, not healthy. But the second part (you need others to mind their business) isn't completely true. That might be part of the reason you may have gotten irritated when your dad said that in your doctor's appointment.

First, there was probably a little truth to what your dad was saying. Maybe you have been a little lazy. When someone points that out, it is irritating. Second, say you're doing everything you can but it's not turning out that well. The last thing you want to hear is how poorly you're doing, especially for something—diabetes—that you didn't want in the first place. Third, the people criticizing you might not be doing their job either. It feels hypocritical. That's irritating. So, let's start with the third reason and see what can be done about this so this irritated feeling doesn't keep coming back, you keep fighting with your parents, and you get burned out. Let's talk about the different kinds of people helping (or "helping") you with your diabetes care.

Different Kinds of Helpers

Throughout the book, I've talked about different people in your family who help you take care of your diabetes. Mother, father, grandparent, sister. There are many others as well—maybe a cousin helps you the most or you live full-time with an aunt or uncle and they help. And stepparents also count—maybe your stepmother is the person who helps the most with your diabetes. The point is that when the word "family" is used, it can mean a lot of different people. The person (or people) who helps you the most to take care of your diabetes is who I want you to think about it as we go through this section.

What kind of helper is that person? Here are a few different kinds of helpers—some more helpful than others.

Diabetes Police

It is probably obvious what this term means. Basically, it is the idea that someone is patrolling nonstop to be sure all the rules are followed. In this case, the person patrols diabetes management and makes sure all the carbs are counted, the precise amount of insulin is given, and there are no extra snacks or desserts that get eaten. And if rules are broken, a citation is issued. You may need to show up in court—your next doctor's visit—while the police officer describes to the court why they had to cite you for inappropriate diabetes management. Punishment is likely to follow.

I know, this is an extreme example, but it illustrates the point. Sometimes people who are genuinely trying to help you take care of your diabetes take it a little too far. This term is something that you may have heard in your doctor's office because healthcare professionals sometimes talk about this with families. It is also on YouTube and other websites. If you search YouTube for "diabetes police," a short video on it will come up. So this is a not a new idea, and there are a lot of people that discuss this. And importantly, it is not usually the most *helpful* kind of helper.

Miscarried Helper

This kind of helper usually starts by trying to offer constructive advice about managing your diabetes, but at some point, it starts being counterproductive. Several psychologists have talked about this over the years and you may have heard about it. What happens in this case is that the helper—let's say a parent—starts off by offering advice about the best way to manage diabetes. Let's even say you follow some or all of that advice. Then, because diabetes is not always predictable or maybe even because the advice wasn't exactly right, you don't achieve the A1c results that this parent expects. The parent may assume you did not follow the advice because the result he expected did not happen. What happens next? You get blamed for the poor result.

So, the end result is the parent feeling frustrated and like you were not doing what you were supposed to. You feel blamed. You and your parent end up in arguments about diabetes. And you may even start doing exactly the opposite of what he suggests or stop doing everything he suggests. In other words, nothing good happens.

Teammate

Clearly, this is the best kind of helper. Probably every type of job that needs to get done or goal that you want to achieve can be done best with teamwork. Several examples outside of diabetes include playing together on a sports team to win a game, dividing up parts of a group project for school, or sharing chores around the house. Even if you are a very independent person, teamwork usually helps to get things done. Taking care of diabetes is the same way. In the next section, we'll talk about the main family relationships you might have at home. Then, several strategies will be reviewed that should help to increase teamwork around diabetes management as well as ways to talk to family members (who may be acting like the Diabetes Police or playing the blame game) about helping with your diabetes.

Parental Help & Tension

The number one reason teens and their parents show up at my office door is because they're fighting a lot. They're having a tough time getting along. Most of the time, this is about diabetes. And it can be about the type of helper the parent is. Or it's about your own difficulties staying organized and being responsible about diabetes (Remember Chapter 5?). Think about the situations on the next page—have you experienced conflict around these things?

It's a safe bet that you've had conflict around these things. The conflict could have started because of you, like the example of fudging your blood sugar number or losing things you need to take care of your diabetes. Your parents might have started the conflict if they are suspicious that you've not been up front with them about food or taking insulin. When there's something very important—like taking care of diabetes—and you have different perspectives, there's bound to be some conflict. Well, here are some strategies for getting rid of that conflict by being better teammates in your diabetes care.

You don't check as many times a day as your parents want.

You get grounded for having an A1c that's too high.

You forgot your insulin at a friend's house and your mom has to drive you back there to get it.

You lost your medic-alert bracelet for the third time.

You told your parents your blood sugar and they don't believe you and want to see the meter.

You told them your blood sugar was 140 when it was really 360. They find out later.

You are high every day after school and your parent asks if you "snuck food".

You have your fourth infection in two months because you're not rotating your injection sites.

You just want a break but no one in your family can help more.

Mom thinks you're depressed, but you think you're just a normal teenager.

Strategies for Increasing Teamwork

Like we discussed before, you've got to have help and support to manage your diabetes. The right kind of support can help you achieve better blood sugars and A1c levels, which will keep you in better shape to have fun doing all the other things you want to do (Chapter 5). The following strategies require some work on your part and as well as you encouraging your parents to do certain things. The strategies include

- avoiding the blame game,
- doing something else besides talking, and
- sharing responsibilities.

Don't play the blame game. In this game, no one ever wins. Both sides leave the game feeling upset, irritated, or burned out. That's why you need to avoid playing this game. You read earlier about the miscarried helper and you've probably felt blamed by a parent. But it can go the other way, too. You may blame your parent for not helping enough and that's why your blood sugars have been so high. Or you blame your parent for "helping" too much, and what you saw as nagging made you want to stop doing something. It's easy to fall in to this trap of blaming the other person.

So, to avoid playing this game, try to do several things.

- First, evaluate the evidence. This is similar to the third step in our problem-solving strategy ("listing the pros and cons"). When you identify some negative result that might be causing conflict (like those in the box earlier in this chapter), take a few minutes and think about the evidence for why it got to this point. You'll eventually notice that is a combination of factors—some about you and some about your parents. For example, if you're arguing about blood sugars, the evidence might be that your parents are on your case a little more than usual, but you're also not checking as much lately because school is really busy.
- Second, come up with a solution that fits the evidence. Once you've identified one thing you're doing and one thing your parents are doing to contribute to conflict, come up with a plan to fix it. You could start this conversation with your parent by saying, "One of the reasons I haven't been checking as much is that I'm feeling a little overwhelmed by school and I'm going to try to focus more on checking my blood sugar by setting a reminder alarm on my phone. I also noticed that you guys have been on my case more about checking and I was hoping that you could try not to remind me as much, at least for the next couple of weeks." You might have to try other things, too, like those discussed below, but it's best to pick one thing and even out the jobs that you and your parents have to do to decrease conflict.

Do something else besides talking. Do you like to talk to your parents? This is not a question about whether you mind telling them about how your day was or what homework you have or where you are going to hang out. This is a question about whether you like talking about your diabetes and particularly your blood sugars, when you gave yourself insulin, and how much food you ate. My guess is that you don't mind talking a little bit about diabetes, but you may not want to talk as much as they do. If that's the case, you may not be able to do the second step of avoiding the blame game by talking. You'll need other strategies besides talking. Take a look at the tips in the box below to see if there are some alternative ways to communicate with your parents.

Other Ways to Communicate With Your Parents

Get a whiteboard and put it on the fridge. Write notes to each other on here. **Nice notes.**

Talk to one of your siblings and see if they're okay with being the middle man and passing information to your parents.

Text or e-mail your parents your recent blood sugar number.

Ask your parent to text you a reminder about checking instead of telling you in person.

If your diabetes nurse is fine with e-mails, both you and your parent can e-mail with numbers and comments separately.

Dedicate a time to sit and discuss diabetes and don't talk about it at other times.

Keep in mind that these tips can keep you from arguing so much with your parents about taking care of diabetes, but they aren't long-term fixes for serious problems you have with your parents. For example, if you try these and keep arguing about diabetes and fight about tons of other things, it's probably worth seeing a therapist to get some help. Therapists work with families, too, and can help to be somewhat of a referee to help you guys figure out how to solve problems. There might be bigger problems beyond diabetes that you need to work out with your parents in the therapist's office.

Share responsibilities. What was one of the first things you learned in preschool or kindergarten? It was probably to share. This is not a tough thing to understand, but it is a tough thing to do. For diabetes, it is important to share diabetes management with your family. Take a look at the questionnaire on page 89 that I have used a lot in working with teenagers and their families. This was made by Dr. Barbara Anderson, who is a psychologist who has worked with thousands of teens with diabetes and their families. For each item, think about who takes more responsibility for doing the task.

Before we get in to how you answered those questions, let's first look at the different tasks involved in managing diabetes. There are quite a few and you probably do not notice them all the time. And there is a chance you do not notice that your parents are doing some things, like picking up prescriptions and making appointments for you. On those items, it would be perfectly normal to note that they are doing them. Also, it may be that certain tasks—deciding what you are going to eat when you go out to dinner—are usually done by just you. Again, that is normal. The problems usually start when someone is doing a certain task or there is disagreement about who is doing it. Mom says, "He is supposed to do it," while you say, "That's Mom's job." That's a full-on blame game.

So, did you have more 1s than 3s or vice versa? Or mostly 2s? This would give you an idea of how much sharing you are doing right now with your parent. The goal is not necessarily to have 2s on everything, but to be sure someone is doing it. In order to be a good sharer and make your preschool teacher proud of you, it is important to

1—decide which tasks you should do, your parents should do, and which ones you will share, and then
2—figure out how to get the jobs done you are going to share.

For example, if you plan to share the job of remembering times to monitor blood sugars, maybe you can suggest to your parents, that they give you one reminder when you are supposed to do it. And if you do not do it within 15 minutes, they can remind you again. There is a lot to remember, so having a plan for sharing can really help.

Sibling Support & Conflict

Like with your parents, there are a lot of things that can cause conflict with siblings, especially when it comes to anything related to your diabetes. Sometimes siblings feel like they don't get as much attention as you

Diabetes Family Responsibility Questionnaire

For each of the following parts of diabetes care, choose the number of the answer that best describes how you and your family generally handle things.

1—I take responsibility for this almost all of the time.
2—My parents and I share responsibility for this about equally.
3—My parents take responsibility for this almost all of the time.

RESPONSIBILITY	YOU	EQUAL	PARENT
Remembering day of clinic appointment.	1	2	3
Telling teachers about diabetes.	1	2	3
Remembering to take morning or evening injection boluses (pump).	1	2	3
Making appointments with dentists or other doctors.	1	2	3
Telling relatives about diabetes.	1	2	3
Taking more or less insulin according to results of blood sugar monitoring.	1	2	3
Noticing differences in health, such as weight changes or signs of an infection.	1	2	3
Deciding what to eat at meals or snacks.	1	2	3
Telling friends about diabetes.	1	2	3
Noticing the early signs of an insulin reaction.	1	2	3
Giving insulin injections or boluses (pump).	1	2	3
Deciding what should be eaten when family has meals out (restaurants, friends' homes).	1	2	3
Carrying some form of sugar in case of an insulin reaction.	1	2	3
Explaining absences from school to teachers or other school personnel.	1	2	3
Rotating injection sites or infusion set-ups (pump).	1	2	3
Remembering times when blood sugar should be monitored.	1	2	3
Checking expiration dates on medical supplies.	1	2	3

Note: Adapted from "Assessing Family Sharing of Diabetes Responsibilities," by B. J. Anderson, W. R. Auslander, K. C. Jung, J. P. Miller, and J. V. Santiago, 1990, *Journal of Pediatric Psychology, 15,* p. 492. Copyright 1990 by Oxford University Press.

or they're not interested in helping with your diabetes management. And this might cause conflict between you and your siblings or more generally in the family. Do any of these sound familiar?

Your brother asks your mom, with you in the room, why you're always getting more attention.

You've asked your sister repeatedly not to tell people about your diabetes, but she keeps doing it.

Your sister has absolutely no interest in helping you, even if you ask.

Your brother is getting sick of being the middle man between you and your parents, even though he was okay with it before.

If you have siblings, chances are you've experienced conflict like in these situations. Before we get in to strategies for getting along better with siblings, let's discuss different ways siblings can be involved in your diabetes care.

You may have an older sibling who substitutes as a parent. Maybe you live with one parent and she works a lot, so the older sibling helps take care of you. Your older brother reminds you about checking and taking insulin and gets on you if you're not keeping up. This could also be a job this sibling is supposed to be doing, but doesn't do it. He spends all of his time at his girlfriend's house and totally blows you off.

Other ways your siblings could be involved in your care (and maybe cause conflict) is if they always go with you to appointments. Perhaps your parents can't find a babysitter so your 8-year-old brother always goes to your appointments. And he always acts like he knows it all and tells your doctor that you keep sneaking cookies. You might also have a younger sibling that clings to you and wants to know everything you're doing...and why. You find this annoying, especially because most of it is about diabetes. It's nice that your younger sister likes to hang out with you and looks up to you, but it's starting to get old and annoying.

Strategies for Increasing Teamwork

What can you do in these situations to avoid conflict? Here are several strategies for avoiding conflict and getting along better with your siblings and family. They include taking their perspective, and educating and involving them.

Take their perspective. When you hear that you get more attention because of your diabetes, your first thought might be *It's not like I wanted diabetes.* That's true, but that can be a hard thing for a sibling to understand. It might be helpful to try and understand their perspective in this case. If you do, you might not feel as defensive or irritated with them when they say something like this. This is especially true for younger siblings because they haven't matured as much as you and have a harder time thinking about how others are feeling. So why do you think a sibling would say something about you getting more attention?

Because of your diabetes, you do spend more time talking to and doing things with your parents. It can be extra preparation to be sure everything is set for a trip or extra calls to the school. The sibling doesn't usually think about any of the reasons for this, just the proof that your parents are giving you a lot of attention. It might help to involve them in some of these activities for two reasons. First, they will get to see what is going on. And second, they may quickly realize it's not all that exciting. It's usually a lot more effective to show things instead of just telling them. They like to see the proof. Try to take your sibling's perspective about your diabetes and they may start to better understand yours.

Educate and involve them. Another reason your sibling might give you a hard time about how much attention you get or generate conflict around diabetes is that they don't understand what's going on. Remember, not knowing something can make it harder to accept and do something about it. It works the same way for your siblings. Try to get them involved and explain what you're doing and why you're doing it. You can even assign them a job. If it's an older sibling, a great job might be to send you a reminder via text message or just tell you to check after school. A younger sibling might be really good at passing on information to your parent, like taking your parent your meter or telling them you need more test strips.

One other thing to consider here is that siblings (and people in general) sometimes react in weird ways to things if they're worried about something.

We've talked about this before with friends—maybe they react weirdly when you tell them you have diabetes because they had an uncle who had diabetes and didn't take care of it. This friend is worried something bad will happen to you. It can be the same thing for siblings. Maybe your sibling saw you have a really low blood sugar or saw you really sick when you were first diagnosed. Perhaps this sibling couldn't really understand what was happening but was really worried about you. This worry may make them feel like you get all the attention or make them stay away from you. But if you educate them and involve them in your diabetes care, they will quickly learn that they don't have anything to worry about. This will especially be true if you're being responsible for your diabetes care, advocating for yourself, and keeping yourself from being burned out. They will see that diabetes can be managed and they will worry less. This will keep them from acting so weird—which is always a great goal for a sibling, don't you think?

An Unsupportive Family

The final family issue to discuss is when you're part of an unsupportive family. Now, this doesn't necessarily mean that your parents or siblings are purposefully being unsupportive. There may be good reasons for less support—you live with a single parent who works two jobs, or you're part of a family where there are several siblings with medical issues, maybe even more serious than diabetes. In that case, both the parents and siblings might have a tough time devoting a ton of time to you and your diabetes. So, when there's a good reason for less support, you may want to try a few things to get more support.

1—Prioritize the support you need. If there are 10 things you need from your parent and it's unlikely they can help you with more than two or three of them, pick the top three and talk with them about those.
2—Be specific in the help you need. Whether it is picking up prescriptions or taking you to an appointment, you've got to be specific in your request.
3—Find some way to be helpful to your parent or sibling. You may end up getting some quality time with them and in the process, help each other out. They get help—maybe it's with making dinner or driving your brother to a friend's house—and they end up finding some time to take you to a movie.

On the other hand, if it doesn't seem like there's a good reason for your parents not being supportive of you and your diabetes care, other strategies might be in order. You may want to try the tips above first and then work toward just directly telling them that you need more help. You may be able to work together as a team to figure out if they can do the job or need to find another family member to help. If it seems like a parent is really struggling with feeling burned out or depressed herself, you may want to suggest to that parent and maybe others in your family that she find some help. If it's related to your diabetes, a therapist in your diabetes center might be able to help. Or you could ask that therapist to help her find someone to see. Parents will be better at helping you if they have done enough to help themselves.

A final thing you might want to try is talking to another adult your parent trusts. You can tell this person, maybe an aunt or uncle, that you're a little worried about your parent and also seem to be slipping with taking care of your diabetes. You can ask them to relay this information to your parent. Your parent may hear it better coming from some other adult.

Putting It All Together

A lot has been covered in this chapter. Hopefully you can move on to the next chapter with the following things in mind. First, it is *your* diabetes but taking care of it should involve teamwork. You can increase the teamwork in your family at the same time you're reducing conflict by avoiding the blame game, having alternatives to talking, and sharing tasks that need to get done. Second, if the people in your life—parents and siblings—aren't good helpers or need to help in a different way, you can suggest some of the strategies listed here or maybe ask a healthcare professional to work with you and your family to come up with a better plan for managing your diabetes. Some of these strategies for being a better team may also help you at school, which is the topic of the next chapter. Also, we'll discuss looking forward to college or a job you plan to start when you're done with high school.

Chapter 8

School Daze

What are the good parts of high school for you? Perhaps it is hanging out with friends between classes, doing well in your classes, or hearing the dismissal bell so you know you're on your way to an extracurricular activity. And you probably view high school as an opportunity to get you moving toward a career, either right after high school or after you've gone to college. Or maybe you can't figure out the good parts of high school and you're not feeling really comfortable. You feel a little lost and overwhelmed and you're struggling to make friends. Plus, you aren't sure what you want to do when you graduate. It can definitely be a challenge to get through high school, especially if you can't find the good parts and don't feel comfortable.

Diabetes adds an extra challenge to high school. From figuring out when and where to do blood sugar checks to having to make up work because you missed it while at a doctor's appointment, diabetes can add some extra hurdles. In order to make it through high school, enjoy your time there, and get yourself ready for the next phase of your life, you've got to tackle those challenges with diabetes. You can do that by getting support from people at school and coming up with solid plans for managing diabetes at school. That's what this chapter is all about. So let's start with a familiar term—your support team—but this time it's about your *school* support team.

School Support Team

This team can include the school nurse, teachers, guidance counselor, principal or vice-principal, and if you're involved in sports, coaches. Like your support team in general, you've got to advocate for yourself and do several things to get the kind of support you need from these people. Take a look at this box to see how this support team can help you in high school.

How to Get the Most out of Your School Support Team

Your diabetes nurse needs more daytime blood sugars, so you ask your school nurse to e-mail (to your other nurse) your lunch-time checks.

Your lunch starts later this semester and you've been going low in the class before lunch (science). Your science teacher lets you eat a snack during class to prevent the low.

You're not crazy about your schedule, so you go to your guidance counselor and ask for a class change. You've planned ahead and know what you want to switch to.

You've missed some important class lectures and discussion because you were at a doctor's appointment. You ask your teacher for an extension to take the test.

You're getting harassed by some other teens about doing an injection in the bathroom. You go to the vice-principal to find a more private place in the school to inject. Maybe his office.

The past few tests in a particular class have been horrible. You need extra help. Go to that teacher or your guidance counselor and ask for extra help.

You just need someone to talk to, so you stop by your favorite teacher's class to talk.

You've got your mind set on a certain career, but aren't sure how to get there. You ask the guidance counselor for advice.

You notice yourself getting burned out with school—can't seem to keep up. Talk to your guidance counselor about alternative classes.

You keep forgetting your Gatorade for sports practice. You ask the coach if he can always keep a few extra around if you forget.

You're annoyed at how little other students know about diabetes, so you ask your health teacher to do a few class lectures on it. You could offer to help or provide examples.

You don't get a ton of support at home, so you ask your school nurse to call your diabetes nurse when you're running out of supplies (at school or at home).

Some are about diabetes and others are just general parts of support you need in high school. Now, you may have gotten help from your school support team in these areas, or maybe you've been too nervous, didn't know who to ask, or you've just been too busy to get the advice you need. Let's go through each support team member and see what you can do to make that a better relationship and get the support you need. With their support, you'll be tackling the challenges of managing diabetes at school in no time.

School Nurse

The school nurse is one of the most important members of your team because this is usually the person you'll interact with the most about your diabetes. Maybe you've had extra help from your school nurse reminding you to check a blood sugar, or she helped problem-solve if your blood sugar was really high one day. As you move in to high school, you may see the nurse less than you did when you were in elementary or middle school because you're expected to be more responsible for yourself as you get older. But if you have access to a school nurse in high school, here are some things to consider when interacting with her:

- Decide what kind of help you need from your school nurse
- Be a good teammate

Decide what you need. Maybe you live in a state where you're not allowed to keep your meter with you and check your blood sugar throughout the day, so you've got to check in the nurse's office. Talk to your nurse, and put it in your Diabetes Management Plan (we'll talk about this soon), about where and when you'll check. Is it your responsibility to stop by or will she find you in between classes? She's also the best person to talk with a teacher who doesn't know much about diabetes and help them understand why you may need to treat a low blood sugar during class. School nurses can also help with plans for sports, gym class, lunch, and helping other people at school understand why you missed some part of class or a test. Identify the help you need and ask for it.

Be a good teammate. As last chapter illustrated, teamwork is the best way to get the help you need. It's easy sometimes to fall into the trap of thinking about your relationship with the school nurse in an adversarial way—maybe you feel like she nags you or doesn't fully understand what it's like to be a high schooler with diabetes. Well, school nurses are required to be part of your diabetes plan at school and they do want to help. If there's some new way you're managing your diabetes, make sure you talk to her about that. If not, you may end up disagreeing about something or it will lead to a misunderstanding. Likewise, if you're not so crazy about being pulled out of lunch to check, then make sure you stop by before lunch to check. If you're taking insulin at school (injections or through the pump), you may have to go to the nurse to do this (even if you are perfectly fine doing this on your own). Try not to get offended, just try to understand that the law or school district requires this. Don't blame the school nurse for something that's out of her hands. Be a good teammate with your nurse.

Teachers

Your school nurse is going to interact with you almost exclusively about diabetes. With these next members of your school support team—teachers—you'll be interacting with them mostly about other things, namely your classes. Here are a few things to try so you can get the most out of your relationships with your teachers in high school.

Explain how diabetes affects your coursework. Diabetes is never an excuse, but it can be a good reason. Take this example. You're in the middle of a test in one of your elective classes—art, music, shop—and you start going low. You've got to do something about this, but it's a timed test. If you miss 10 minutes, you won't finish in time. Diabetes doesn't excuse you from the test, but it is a good reason to make it up. (Hopefully this is part of your 504 Plan, which we'll talk about soon.) You can see how educating your teachers about your diabetes can help you avoid conflicts over needing more time or needing to retake a test. Plus, if a teacher has a strict rule about no snacks in the class, you may need to get special permission to carry your fast-acting sugary snack with you and use it if necessary. Perhaps you're in a vocational-technical high school and you're constantly working with electrical devices or tools. You want to be sure you don't go low and have that sugary drink with you at all times. You'll find that teachers are usually pretty reasonable about these things if you bring it up before they happen.

Consult them for real-world advice. Your teachers can be good members of your school support team in general, too. Are you struggling to figure out what you want to do? Ask your teachers if they always wanted to do what they're doing and find out how they got in to teaching. You may have a teacher who worked in a certain field—construction contractor or professional dancer—for a long time before teaching. There are different pathways to get to where you want to be or to do what you want to do. This may also help you to feel a little less stressed about decisions you have to make about what you're going to do after high school. Try different classes and talk to teachers with real-world experience to see what your options are.

Counselors

Counselors in school are usually either guidance counselors, who help with classes and career planning; school psychologists, who help with classes but also work like a therapist, helping with school adjustment; or they are both. Depending on who is available to you, these are some things that you may want to talk with your counselor about.

Talk about getting the most out of high school. One of the reasons teens can feel uncomfortable in high school is because they haven't found some class or subject that really interests them. You might have been put in a certain track and only have access to certain classes. But if you talk to your counselor about this, maybe you can find a new class that is more interesting to you. It's high school and it's perfectly fine (and normal) if you haven't settled on a career path. Try to get different experiences and then figure out what you want to do after you graduate later. You may find an undiscovered talent by trying a new class.

Talk about career paths. You may also feel uncomfortable in high school because you're not sure what's next for you and other teens seem like they've got it all figured out. Perhaps your family hasn't given you much guidance or they've just assumed you'll choose the same career they did. Or you just might not know what your options are. Talk to your counselor at school. They can review different career paths and also can give you different tests that tell you what careers you may be good at. If you're unsure of what's next, you might feel anxious and end up avoiding thoughts about it. If you get more information and figure out your options, you'll be less anxious.

Get help if you're feeling burned out. You can get burned out about high school almost as easily as you can get burned out about diabetes. It's something you have to do nearly every day and sometimes you feel like you keep doing the same thing over and over again, and it's getting you nowhere. It's really tough, too, if you don't feel like you fit in at school. But you can use some of the same things to avoid high school burnout that you use to avoid diabetes burnout. You can always talk to the guidance counselor or school psychologist when you feel like you're not going anywhere in high school or you're having a hard time socially. You may need to try resetting things, trying something new, or having a regular time to talk with your counselor about what's going on. You'll find ways to keep high school burnout from creeping up. Remember, you've got to advocate for yourself to avoid burnout. Do the same here and get the support you need.

Principal

Your principal and vice-principal will likely be the least involved of your school support team members, but they have several important roles.

- They are in charge of the school, so they should be aware of your diabetes and have policies in place to help you manage your diabetes at school. If that's not the case, you may want to talk to him to see if something can be done to make your experience better.
- Principals can be good advocates for you around your diabetes. For instance, the principal might be able to find alternative places to do shots. He also might be interested in making sure those kids aren't harassing you (or anyone else, for that matter).
- The principal is the person to talk to if you're trying to get a fund-raiser done at school. Maybe you're interested in raising money for the JDRF or another diabetes association.

A team effort at advocating for diabetes (and yourself) can be really successful.

Coaches

If you're involved in sports at your school, your coaches are members of your support team. Their job is obviously to coach the team, but they also are in charge of making sure the players are safe while doing that sport. That means they need to know about your diabetes and know how they can help you if that's necessary. For example, we've talked about how coaches might remind you to check your blood sugar or make sure you have a fast-acting sugary snack with you at all times, but there's more to it.

- Your coach may be able to tell when you're not performing well physically. It's very hard to do anything, physical or mental, when your blood sugar is high. Your coach might be able to pick up on that and suggest that you take a break and check your blood sugar.

- Your coach can also help you with athletic scholarships and recruiting if you want to play sports in college.
- Your coach can also work with you to make sure that other players don't pick on you or treat you differently because of your diabetes. You can advocate for yourself by telling the coach not to give you any special treatment (outside of what we just talked about regarding your diabetes).

Taking Diabetes to School

We've talked a lot so far about how to get the help you need from your school support team, but what about the basics of taking care of your diabetes at school? If you've worked closely with your support team members, this part will be much easier. You'll have support for these things. But let's look at a few specific things to consider when taking care of your diabetes at school.

Diabetes Management Plan

You need to have a Diabetes Management Plan for school. This is usually a one-page document that describes what you need to do at school to take care of your diabetes. Examples of this can be found on several websites listed in the Resources section of this book. Two things that will definitely be on this plan are checking blood sugars and injecting insulin. Work with your support team—school nurse, teachers, coaches—to identify when you'll check and where. And what will you do if your blood sugar is high? Have a specific plan in place—how much insulin you'll take, at what number your diabetes nurse or doctor will be called, and other specific things you need to be sure you've got under control. You may also write more specific steps in to your plan, like you'll text your parent your blood sugar at lunch time.

Plus, like Chapter 2 suggested ways to be a good advocate, you need to be part of making up your plan for school. Don't leave it up to your parents or school personnel to decide. Speak up and make sure it works for you. If there's something in there you don't like, you're probably not going to do it. Work together as a team to put a plan in place that's going to work. Be sure your school nurse talks to your diabetes nurse to get all the up-to-date information about your diabetes management.

Accommodations

Because you have diabetes, you have the right to have something called a 504 Plan. Its name comes from Section 504 of the Rehabilitation Act that was put into place in 1973. Basically, it gives students in public schools the right to have certain accommodations because of a number of things, one of them being diabetes. Accommodations are extra things that help the student be as successful as possible. So, you may have accommodations as part of a 504 Plan, like being able to leave class when you need to for diabetes-related reasons. Plus, if you miss class due to a low blood sugar, you can make up the work. There are other accommodations, but the bottom line is that there are ways the law advocates for you because you have diabetes and need some extra support to take care of it at school. Make sure you take advantage of this.

Now, if you're in a private high school, it gets a little trickier. You can still have this plan, but the school doesn't have to respect it. That's because the law allowing the 504 Plan only applies to schools that get money from the state or federal government (in other words, public schools). It doesn't mean you can't go to a private school if you have diabetes, it just means that you'll want to check what types of accommodations the school will give you, if they give any, outside of a specific 504 Plan. (Your principal and guidance counselor can help you identify these accommodations.) This is usually easier to figure out in high school than if you were still in elementary or middle school.

Extracurriculars

The final part to cover in this chapter is taking diabetes to your extracurricular activities. These could be sports, an internship for one of your classes, clubs, drama, or anything else that's connected to a school-related function. It's good to get yourself involved in extracurricular activities because it helps you meet new teens, gives you a chance to experience new things, and showcases how you can manage diabetes and do grown-up things at the same time (Remember Chapter 5?). But what are some things that can keep you back and what are ways to overcome them?

You feel like you don't fit in. You may feel like you don't fit in to any of the extracurricular activities and that's why you're not doing them. You're not especially athletic, don't really like acting or playing music, and you're not crazy about committing to something new that you might not like. Go to the guidance counselor or a teacher that runs a club (or several) and describe your interests. They can help you find something you'll fit in to. Talk to your friends as well—they know you well and might be able to help you figure out an activity that's right for you.

And don't let your diabetes keep you from doing something. Your parents and diabetes support team want you to enjoy your time in high school and will help you figure out ways to adjust your diabetes schedule to fit these activities. And you can use the same tips from above when doing these extracurricular activities.

Start your own group. If you can't find a certain group or club that fits your interests or none seem like they'd be flexible around your diabetes, start your own. You may be surprised at how many other teens are interested in the same thing. You could start a topic or group discussion online and find others who are interested. Or you could post flyers around school, on bulletin boards, or just talk to people. Get the word out!

Putting It All Together

If you take advantage of help from your school support team and find ways to take care of diabetes at school, the good parts of high school will become clear and you'll feel much more comfortable. Whether it's the school nurse or a teacher, work together with them on your Diabetes Management Plan and any extra ways (in other words, accommodations) you can be more successful with your diabetes in high school. This is a crucial time for deciding what you like and what you want to do next, and being successful with your diabetes will make it easier to figure those things out. Now, we're moving on to other topics that high schoolers have to deal with—alcohol and drugs, and relationships and sex. The next chapter is about alcohol and drugs and provides some guidelines for using them (if you decide to) as well as how your diabetes is affected by alcohol and drugs.

Chapter 9

Alcohol & Drugs

Most teenagers are presented with the opportunity to drink alcohol or use drugs. These opportunities can come up when out with friends, at home when your parents are out of town, or on a school trip. Now, you may or may not take advantage of those opportunities. Whether you do will depend on your feelings, beliefs, and the situations you find yourself in. While I, your doctor and nurse, and your parents and other caregivers prefer and suggest that you wait until you are of legal age and only engage in legal activities, if you do decide to drink or use drugs, you should know what you're getting into and be prepared so you can be safe. Again, like everything else in the book, because you have diabetes, there are a few extra things to consider if you find yourself in a position to drink or use drugs. But before we get in to the facts about alcohol and drugs, as well as what effects they have on your body because you have diabetes, let's talk about the myths of alcohol and drug use. Take a look at some of the most common misconceptions about alcohol and drugs on the next page. They might ring a bell.

Myth Busters: Alcohol & Drugs

MYTH	REALITY
Everybody drinks.	The Centers for Disease Control (CDC) report that 45% of high schoolers report drinking alcohol in the past month. That leaves 55% who weren't drinking.
Everybody smokes pot.	Even fewer smoke pot than drink alcohol. About 6% of 8th-graders, 14% of 10th-graders, and 19% of 12th-graders report using marijuana in the month before a survey.
Ecstasy is really popular.	Since Ecstasy came on the scene, the number of high schoolers using it has dropped—from about 11% in 2003 to 6% in 2007.
Marijuana is not addictive.	There is evidence that you can become dependent on marijuana, because when you quit, you have withdrawal symptoms. It can be addictive.
Smoking pot is harmless.	The active agent in pot, THC, can cause damage to your brain cells. Plus, regular pot smokers have the same breathing problems as people who smoke cigarettes.
Alcohol gives me energy.	Alcohol is technically a depressant, not a stimulant. So it actually slows the body down instead of speeding it up (and giving you energy).
Alcohol makes sex better.	Alcohol doesn't make sex better. It does reduce inhibitions, so you may want to have sex more, but alcohol actually reduces sensitivity and reduces your ability to perform sexually.
I can sober up quickly.	When you drink alcohol, the only thing that sobers you up is time. Drinking coffee, taking a cold shower, or something else won't sober you up more quickly. It might make you feel more alert, but your blood alcohol content (BAC) is still high.

So, now that we've clarified some misconceptions, let's move on to the facts.

Alcohol: The Facts

The myths and their realities above were presented for two reasons. First, as we've discussed several times before in the book, knowledge is power. Knowing the facts helps you make better decisions. Second, knowing the facts might help you feel less pressured to do something you don't want to do, especially if the pressure comes from *Hey, everybody's doing it and nothing bad will happen*. So, what are the facts about alcohol and diabetes? There are two major issues here:

- Alcohol impairs your judgment, so it impairs your ability to take care of your diabetes and to do things you normally do, like drive or talk.
- Drinking will increase your chance of having very low blood sugars.

Here's why these things happen. When alcohol is consumed—surely in someone above the legal drinking age—it quickly moves into the bloodstream. Alcohol affects the entire body, but the liver takes charge of breaking down the alcohol. Just like anything that there is more of than can be taken care of—too much water in a container and it overflows, too many texts in your inbox and no more texts can be received—if the liver cannot keep up with how quickly alcohol gets in to the body, the person will start to feel "buzzed" and may become drunk. When you're buzzed or drunk, the parts of your brain that control your judgment and impulses become impaired. This is gradual, but because you're drinking, you don't usually notice these changes. Then, you find yourself in a situation where you're not making the best decisions. For diabetes, this can mean ignoring symptoms of low or high blood sugars, not checking enough, or taking too much insulin. In general, you may find yourself in a situation where you're doing something sexually you wouldn't normally do, driving while drunk, or saying things that you'll regret.

Now back to the liver. One of the other jobs of the liver is to keep a nice balance of sugar in the blood. So, if you are going low, the liver will respond and release glucose in to the blood. Even without alcohol, when you are going low, the liver is not going to release enough sugar so you should always treat a low blood sugar. When someone is drinking alcohol, this job of the liver takes a back seat to breaking down the alcohol. In other words, the liver stops releasing glucose in to the blood stream. So, how is that dangerous? You probably guessed it. Your risk of having a low blood sugar goes up when you drink alcohol because your liver isn't pitching in that extra sugar. And this might not show up right away. For example, you may drink a lot of alcohol and check your blood sugar before going to bed. Even if it's normal then or close to the range you want, there's a great chance it will drop lower and lower as the night goes on. Remember, your body is still working to get the alcohol out of your system long after you've stopped drinking.

These are the facts about alcohol and diabetes. Drinking alcohol may not be an interest of yours now or in the future, but you should be prepared in case you do want to drink. No matter how old you are, these will still be the facts about alcohol and diabetes.

Reminders About Drinking

Here are some reminders if you decide to drink, even though you are not of legal age and it's not recommended that you do:

- Always have someone (sober) in your group who knows you have diabetes and knows what to do if something comes up.
- Wear your medical ID bracelet. Everyone knows it's not super-fashionable, but wear it every time you drink.
- Always have food before you drink. You should never drink on an empty stomach.
- Drink in moderation. For example, adults are encouraged to drink no more than 1–2 alcoholic drinks each day. That is the textbook definition of moderation. The American Diabetes Association has the same recommendation for adults with diabetes.
- Pace yourself. Binge drinking is not a good idea, so if you're not doing the moderation thing, spread out drinks over an extended period of time, so your liver can try to keep up.
- Pay attention to how many carbs you are getting when you drink alcohol. You should talk with your diabetes doctor or nurse (yes, even though you're underage) to see what they suggest. Often people with diabetes try not to drink sugary alcoholic drinks and they usually do not take extra insulin for the carbs in alcohol.
- Alcohol is loaded with carbs. Light beers, non-sugary drinks, or distilled liquor with diet, no-cal mixers, may be advised by your doctor or nurse over sugary drinks.

Marijuana: The Facts

What happens with blood sugars when I smoke pot? How does it affect diabetes?
Many teens with diabetes, not just the ones I see in therapy, have these questions about marijuana and diabetes. I always give an answer but also tell the person asking the question to ask their diabetes doctor or nurse. But before I get to that, here are some basic facts about pot's influence on you in general:

- Using marijuana puts you at risk for all of the problems that come along with doing something illegal. You could get caught with it, get arrested, and maybe have to pay a fine.
- Smoking can make it harder to breathe and will do damage to your lungs.
- Pot impairs your judgment. Doing the things you normally do after you have used marijuana will change how you do them. Attempting to drive after smoking marijuana is not a good idea.

And for the effects of pot on you because you have diabetes…

- Pot will impair your ability to appropriately coordinate carb counting, taking insulin, and knowing what your blood sugar is. The result will likely be high blood sugars.
- If you eat pot in something, like a brownie, you're going to face the same chance of high blood sugars later.

But what does marijuana do to blood sugars? Unlike alcohol, there does not appear to be a direct impact on blood sugars when marijuana is used. There is nothing that happens with the liver like there is with alcohol. When this has been studied in a laboratory, marijuana usually does not directly change what blood sugars are—the operative word being *directly*. The way that marijuana affects blood sugars is that after using it, people are usually impaired. They do not have the same ability to count carbs and adjust insulin levels. This is a big problem with marijuana because a lot of people get the "munchies" after using it. It is pretty straightforward at that point. Eat too much because you are hungry, don't give yourself enough insulin, and your blood sugar goes very high. There are also dangers of going low if you misjudge and overcompensate with too much insulin.

So, one of the issues with using marijuana is that it impairs your ability to take care of your diabetes. The other issues apply to everyone with or without diabetes—it is illegal, impairs your judgment, and you can do long-term damage to your lungs if you smoke marijuana.

Reminders About Pot

If you choose to smoke (or eat) pot, even though I don't think you should, here are some reminders to keep you safe:

- Always have someone (not high) in your group who knows you have diabetes and knows the drill in case you can't care for yourself.
- Set a time to check your blood sugar, agree to have your sober friend(s) remind you, and do it.
- Try to avoid high blood sugars by eating and doing your normal routine (carb counting and taking insulin) before smoking. This may help to keep the munchies in check later.
- Wear your medical ID bracelet.
- Again, moderation is best. However, because smoking (or using) pot is illegal, there aren't guidelines for it like there are with alcohol for adults. So, if you're going to smoke pot, do not do it on a regular (daily or multiple times a week) basis.
- Always know where the pot came from. There are plenty of stories about people smoking pot that is laced with some other drug. Don't smoke something if you don't know where it came from (e.g., don't smoke a joint that is passed at a concert).

Other Drugs

The basics about using any illegal drug (or abusing prescription drugs) are the same—you could get caught, it can impair your ability to do things, and it may cause you physical harm. In every case of using any other drug, having diabetes increases your chance of having something bad happen. For these illegal and prescription drugs, there may be direct and indirect effects.

For example, you may take an "upper" to be more alert or have more energy. In general, these types of drugs (amphetamines and stimulants) will increase adrenaline in your system and that's usually associated with a rise in blood sugar levels. So, you may be more alert and energized, but your blood sugar is also rising. That's a direct effect. On the other hand, you may use something like Ecstasy, which again may cause this feeling of having endless energy, but there's not much of a direct effect. Instead, you don't feel hungry, skip meals, and don't pay attention to your blood sugars. Eventually, you end up low and need help treating the low. Finally, you may use a substance that you don't know how it will affect you. Maybe it causes you to pass out. You did not check blood sugars earlier and did not know you were trending low. While passed out, you do not catch your low blood sugar and actually end up with a very serious hypoglycemic episode. Not only are these situations risky for your health, but they are also scary.

The use of illegal drugs and abusing prescription drugs can have direct and indirect effects on you and your blood sugars. It's of course best to not use these drugs or engage in prescription drug abuse.

Reminders About Drug Use

If you decide to use drugs, which are illegal and very dangerous for you to use, remember these things:

- Know what you're taking. There are tons of ways to figure this out, from asking a reliable person you're with to searching the Internet. You could punch in a description of the pill to Google and find out what it is, what it does, and what might happen to you because of your diabetes. Do not take something if you're unsure what it is.
- Make sure you're with someone sober who knows you have diabetes. And make sure this person knows what you took.
- Try the drug in a controlled environment. Know who is around, where you are, and that your car keys are locked up.
- If you're using a prescription medication illegally, you may want to seek help from a doctor or therapist (or both) to stop. It can be really hard to stop this once you start.
- Again, wear your medical ID bracelet.

Tobacco

We've talked about alcohol, pot, and some other drugs, but another dangerous drug is nicotine. It's the active agent in cigarettes and smokeless tobacco (chew). Nicotine is highly addictive and has several direct and indirect effects on you because of your diabetes.

- Nicotine acts as a stimulant and can cause some of the same things to happen that were described before. In short, it will cause a rise in blood sugars.
- Nicotine causes high blood pressure by constricting your arteries. So, your heart has a harder time pumping blood throughout the body. This is dangerous for everybody, but especially dangerous for a person with diabetes. This is because diabetes (and not controlling it) can cause buildup in your arteries, making it harder for blood to move through. So, if you're using nicotine, it can accelerate damage to your body.
- Smoking cigarettes causes damage to your lungs and will make it harder to breathe. When this happens, you may feel less like you want to exercise and stay healthy. Those things present big problems for your diabetes indirectly because you're likely to not take as good care of yourself as you should.

With all of these things in mind, it's easy to see why there aren't guidelines for using nicotine. It's best not to start. If you have, ask for help to stop. There are good medications that can help you lose your addiction to nicotine and you can also work with a therapist to do this.

Peer Pressure

How many "don't give in to peer pressure" speeches or lectures have you heard? Probably a lot—at school, home, camp, or some religious group you're part of. This peer pressure section won't take up too much of your time. Basically, there are three things to keep in mind when you're feeling pressured to do drugs, drink, or really anything else that you might come across in your teenage years:

1—Try to identify why you're feeling pressured.
2—Know why the other person is pressuring you.
3—Know your choices.

Let's look at each of these ideas, how they relate, and how they can help you deal with peer pressure.

Identify why you're feeling pressured. We've talked a lot about making level-headed and informed decisions in this book. When you're presented with the opportunity to drink or do drugs, slow things down and try to figure out why you're feeling pressured before you make a decision to use. It might be that you're around a new group of teens and you want to fit in. You've struggled making new friends and you don't want to miss the opportunity to find some teens to hang out with. It could be that you're curious about a certain drug because you've heard an older sibling talk about it. Or you're feeling stressed out in general and you think trying something will help you calm down.

Understand why the other person is pressuring you. Is she just pressuring you because she wants to feel more like she fits in, too? If someone else is doing it with her, she feels better. Or it could just be a regular thing for this person and there's not a lot of pressure, just an assumption that you do it. Perhaps the other person is doing it because they're stressed out and they say, "Let's kick back, get high, and just not worry about anything."

Figure out your choices. You can do this by using the information about you and the person pressuring you. Obviously, it's not as simple as *to use or not to use*. It's more complex than that. So try to line up why you're feeling pressured to do it and why the other person is pressuring you. If it's because you both want to fit in, don't do it. Walk away and find another way to feel like you fit in. If you're feeling stressed, don't do it. It will just be a quick fix and your problems will be there when you come back to reality. You should only do something if you have some interest in it, know how to do it safely, and preferably, do it when you're of legal age.

Peer pressure speech over.

Putting It All Together

A lot of information has been reviewed in this chapter, but one of the main ideas is that you should be informed, prepared, and smart when it comes to drinking or using drugs. Try to figure out why you're feeling pressured and why others are pressuring you before you decide to use. Also, know what to expect from all the different drugs reviewed in this chapter. It's certainly best to wait until you're of legal age (if the drug is legal at all) because you're physically and mentally more mature. But if you decide to try these things earlier, know the facts and be prepared for situations that come up. When you are prepared, the chances of making good choices go up. Now it's time for another important topic, and one that's likely on your mind as a teenager, relationships and sex.

Chapter 10

Relationships & Sex

If you skipped directly to this chapter, make sure you go back and read everything else in the book because you will not pass the test at the end of the book. This is obviously just a joke—there is no test at the end of the book. But some of the information in this chapter may be more interesting than other parts of the book. It may be more interesting because these are topics you are thinking about or because, for some reason or another, no one has talked to you about these things. Or you're struggling to see how diabetes can fit in to your dating relationships and what sex is going to be like because of diabetes. This part of the book deals with sex in general as well as everything about sex that is affected by and affects diabetes. We'll start with hormones and then move on to dating and sex. We'll also focus on the emotional aspects of relationships and sex because your emotions play a big part in decisions you'll make and the quality of the romantic relationships you form.

Raging Hormones

Growth spurts. Acne. Mood swings. Hormones can be nasty for every teen. Just when you thought they'd done enough, hormones—like estrogen and testosterone—do another number on your diabetes. Yep, they can significantly affect your blood sugars, how much insulin you need, and just your overall diabetes control. We'll start with the biology of raging hormones and then see how these hormones and other changes can cause emotional ups and downs.

By now, you've probably heard a lot about puberty or experienced it yourself. As the hormone estrogen (in girls) or testosterone (in guys) increases, you'll experience a number of changes with your diabetes. For example, these hormonal changes cause you to be less sensitive to insulin. So, what usually happens? You need more insulin and you probably see some spikes in your blood sugars. You may have been on a smaller dose of insulin when you were 12 and then by 14, it's much higher. Now, it can be worrisome to you if you keep increasing your insulin doses—*When's it ever going to stop increasing?!* Try to understand that this is temporary—your raging hormones won't cause these changes forever. Usually, by the time you're finishing up high school and getting in to your early 20s, the amount of insulin you need starts to even out. This is especially true if your diabetes control is good.

What about the blood sugar spikes? Well, these are tied in to your raging hormones, too, and you may not have enough insulin in your body. So, be prepared and do something about it. Here's what you can do:

- Check your blood sugar more often when you're seeing these spikes. That can be helpful for treating high blood sugars but also gives your diabetes doctor and nurse good information to adjust your insulin doses.
- Exercise. Physical activity is really good for your body because it helps increase insulin sensitivity and helps your body use your injected insulin more effectively (Remember Chapter 5?). And obviously, this helps you stay healthy, too.

Beyond the changes you see in your body because of these hormones, they can also affect your emotions. Do you get through the day just fine, maybe even pretty happy, and then get home and as soon as a parent says something to you, you snap? You yell and get kinda nasty. Well, this strong emotional response could be related to your hormones. Or maybe you feel really depressed and can't figure out why—everything is going well for you. Well, it could be because your body is producing a huge amount of these hormones and it's a little out of whack (to be really technical about it). This usually calms down within a little while, so try to do something to get your mind off of it. If it seems to be happening a lot, talk to your doctor or nurse about it. We'll talk a little more in a bit about other emotions that come along with puberty and hormonal changes in your body.

Menstruation & Birth Control

For the same reason discussed above, girls may see some changes in their blood sugars around menstruation. Basically, this has to do with the surge of hormones (estrogen and progesterone) that occurs when you're entering this cycle. If you notice anything, it will be a rise in blood sugars. The same tips would apply here—check a little more often and talk with your doctor or nurse about it.

Now, if you're thinking about using birth control, you definitely need to talk to your diabetes doctor and nurse. One, you'll need them to get a prescription, and two, they will know the best options because you have diabetes. They also can talk with you about your interest in sexual activity and being safe (we'll talk more about that soon). You may want birth control for a couple reasons. The first is pretty clear, as a contraceptive device to avoid getting pregnant. The other can be because you need to regulate your menstrual cycle. Some of the birth control pills have extra benefits (because they are hormones) like treating acne. Again, it's important to talk to your doctor about all of the reasons you want birth control.

Testosterone

What about you guys? Well, you obviously don't have the same pattern (usually monthly) of hormone surges as girls, but you've got some things to pay attention to yourself. In some ways, because your surges are a little less predictable, you need to stay on top of it even more. For example, testosterone significantly increases your level of aggression and your "sex drive." You may feel really worked up at different times and aren't sure why. These surges will usually pass, but it's good to find things to do when they're happening. Take your frustration and aggression out on a safe target—maybe by doing a sport or doing some physical activity on your own. Regular levels of physical activity will help these surges a lot. And they do even out over time, but it may be a little while so you need to find good, and safe, outlets for this extra energy.

Dating With Diabetes

Now for the interesting stuff. Dating and relationships for teens are tough (and awkward) enough without throwing diabetes into the mix. From taking insulin on a dinner date to figuring out when is the best time to tell the person you're seeing about your diabetes, there are plenty of things to think about because you have diabetes. Plus, you may feel a little nervous about starting a relationship or have been flat-out rejected because of your diabetes. Well, this section covers a lot of those issues and will hopefully give you the confidence to date because you'll have some ways to talk about and deal with your diabetes during a romantic relationship.

Talk About Your Diabetes

Previous parts of the book have talked about meeting new people and telling them about your diabetes or telling old friends who don't know about your diabetes (Chapter 6). But we didn't cover anything about talking about diabetes when you're romantically interested in or involved with someone. Some of the same tips apply. You'll want to plan ahead and practice what you'll say, but there are other specific things that you might want to say when you're on that first date (or whatever numbered date you decide to tell your girl- or boyfriend). Check out the box on the next page for some specific situations and ways to talk about your diabetes. You can work in some humor or just go straight at it, as long as you talk about it in a way you're comfortable with.

What did you notice about these responses? Well, they all involved telling the other person you have diabetes, but they were all a little bit different in *how* you did it. Remember, you've got to find a way that you're comfortable talking about your diabetes. If you get a strange look or response when you tell the other person, give them another chance. They just might not understand. Describe it a little more. But if they end up not wanting to be with you because of diabetes (by the way, this is pretty unlikely), you're better off without them.

Plan Your Dates Wisely

Besides figuring out a way to tell the person you're interested in or dating about your diabetes, you should also plan your dates wisely. Here are a few things to keep in mind:

- Be part of the planning. The best way to plan for what you'll need to bring is to know what you'll be doing.
- If you can't be part of the planning because your date wants to surprise you, be prepared by bringing a larger bag (or keeping extra supplies in your car).

Scripts for Talking About Diabetes

SITUATION	RESPONSE
You pick up your date and she sees test strips on the passenger seat of your car. You were going to wait to tell her, but you go ahead anyway.	Those are test strips. I have type 1 diabetes and have to check my blood sugar. Don't worry, it's not contagious.
You need to do an injection at dinner, but you've already gone to the bathroom (go again, he might think you're strange).	I have diabetes and need to do an insulin injection. Will it bother you if I do it at the table? It will be really quick.
You ask the guy you're interested in dating if he wants to grab something to eat after school. He says, "Don't you have diabetes? I thought you had to watch what you eat."	Yep, but I've got it covered. Do you still want to go? (This applies only if you're still interested.)
This is the first time you're being intimate with your girlfriend. She notices your pump tubing and says, "What's that? Are you hooked up to something?"	It's my insulin pump. I have diabetes. I probably should've told you earlier, but it's really not a big deal.
You're on Facebook and you ask a friend out. She says, "Sure, but tell me more about you. You don't have much on your profile." So you send her a separate message (not on her wall).	I have diabetes, got it when I was 5, kinda annoying, but I deal with it.
You're at the beach with a guy you're interested in. He sees a bruise on your abdomen and asks how you got it. It's from an injection gone wrong.	Oh, I was doing an insulin injection—I have diabetes—and messed up. No big deal.
You ask your girlfriend what she knows about diabetes. She says, "Not much. Why?"	Well, I have type 1 diabetes and I can tell you about it if you want.
You're out to dinner and you're staying away from the dessert your boyfriend just ordered because your blood sugar is high. He asks why.	I didn't tell you, but I have type 1 diabetes and I usually try not to go overboard with desserts. I'll eat just a little bit.

- If it's an all-day date, keep some snacks with you and a fast-acting sugary drink or snack.
- If you're going to be doing something active, plan ahead. Maybe you want to reduce your insulin dose for the day (like your nighttime Lantus dose or lower your basal rate in your pump) or just be sure you have a bunch of extra snacks with you.
- Find convenient times to check. If you don't want to be out in the open about it, do it when he runs to the bathroom or when you go to the bathroom.
- If you think the date may end up in some sexual activity, make sure you know how to handle your diabetes in those situations (we'll review more soon). Actually, no matter if you think it will end up in sexual activity or not, be prepared and be safe. (For example, use a condom.)

Sex, Sex, Sex

Be informed, be prepared, and be smart. This phrase is relevant to sex as well as many other areas in your life. Being informed means that you have the facts. Being prepared means that you are ready to handle situations that come up. Being smart means that you make good choices.

No matter how "sex" is used, it comes up a lot in the life of a teenager. It can be discussions in the halls at school about how "hot" someone is. It may be watching any number of TV shows targeted at teens that have multiple story lines about sex—maybe there is a couple that is hooking up and then one cheats on the other. There are also other shows that focus on consequences of having sex—getting pregnant—and other young adult oriented shows that focus on promiscuous behavior. In other words, sleeping around.

It is a normal part of development to become increasingly interested in sex as you get older. Part of this is biologic—hormones are changing and new ones are developing (like we discussed earlier). Part of this is social and cultural—there is a lot about sex that shows up on an everyday basis. It is also normal to feel a little weird talking about sex with adults. That is often why so much "sex ed" happens with friends—they are easier to talk with about it. You should know, though, that friends do not always have the right facts. That's why it is important to be informed by under-standing the true facts and not just relying on friends or other teenagers to teach you sex ed. Let's start with your sex options.

Your Sex Options

In general, teens have several options for sexual activity. One is to completely avoid it—you know this as abstinence. There are a number of teenagers who follow this guideline and do not engage in sexual activity. Even if this is the option you choose, you should still be informed, prepared, and smart about sexual activity. There is also the option of engaging in certain sexual behaviors but not all of them. Finally, someone could be involved in all aspects of sexual activity, including intercourse.

There are a number of studies that show that sex ed helps keep teens safer with regard to sex. If you go to the Centers for Disease Control website (www.cdc.gov), you will be able to find all kinds of statistics and information on this topic. There are a lot of numbers and information, but it may be helpful to read about what other teens are doing and how they can be safer when engaging in sexual behaviors. Also, there are a lot of websites about sex ed that also give you opportunities to chat with other teens. One really good website is Sex, etc. (www.sexetc.org). It offers a ton of information on the topic. It is worth reading. Basically, if you know the facts, you are prepared. When you are prepared, you can be smart by making good choices.

One important thing to remember, for all the guys and girls reading this, is that you should never engage in sexual activity unless *you* want to. In other words, maybe you're getting pressure to have sex from your testosterone-raging boyfriend. If you're not ready, explain that you aren't and tell him your limits. Girls can also put the pressure on you, but it's less common. But the same rule applies—don't do it until you're ready. Being ready means that you've thought about the consequences and are prepared to handle them.

Sex & Diabetes

There are usually no significant sexual problems that happen during this time because of diabetes. Now, some teenagers may worry, though, because they have heard of adults having sexual problems because of diabetes. One of the main issues is that uncontrolled blood sugars and long periods of time with high A1c values can cause problems with how blood flows through your body. When this happens, the smallest blood vessels are at higher risk for being hurt. This is why people with diabetes some times develop problems with their eyes and feet—these places have really small blood vessels.

Sexual organs can be affected by this, too. Yep, we're talking about the penis and vagina. For you guys, maybe you've seen one of the thousands of commercials on TV for medications for erectile dysfunction (ED). ED definitely sounds like something you don't want to get, right? Well, it is a concern for adult men, and particularly for adult men with diabetes, because uncontrolled and high blood sugars for long periods of time damage these small blood vessels. But you can avoid this by taking care of your diabetes.

Now, for both guys and girls, the other way that diabetes can affect sex is out-of-range blood sugars. This is the same as any other physical activity. What happens when you try and walk, run, or jog and your blood sugar is low? You may feel out-of-energy, slowed down, or even get some cramps in the muscles in your legs. You may also feel worn out or unable to perform at your best when your blood sugar is really high. Our bodies will perform best when blood sugars are in a good range. Now, the range is set by your doctor and nurse, but is probably something like 80–180. Maybe a little higher, but not much.

If you go much higher, you're in for some problems sexually, too. If you're doing any kind of sexual activity and your blood sugar is really high, you're not going to perform well. This may even set you up for an embarrassing situation. Maybe the sexual encounter ends more rapidly than you wanted or you get tired very quickly. You could feel ashamed about it and avoid doing that again. You might even worry that your partner will tell his or her friends. Obviously, this isn't a cool thing to do, but it might happen. If you keep you blood sugars in a good range—not too low and not too high— you'll be better off when you want to do something sexually.

When You Have a Pump

Can you imagine your boyfriend or girlfriend saying this? *Wow, your pump is so sexy. I'm so glad we're about to have sex.* Probably not. If you're on a pump, you may have found yourself in a situation where the pump itself, its tubing, or the location of the insertion site gets in the way of being intimate with your partner. Here are some ways to avoid a potentially awkward situation:

- Tell your boyfriend or girlfriend about your diabetes and how you manage it. (This is what we've talked about so far.) Maybe even explain a little about the pump and how it works.
- Come up with a plan to avoid the pump getting in the way (and you resenting your pump for it). Now, you don't usually want to

be disconnected from your pump for very long. Your doctor and nurse will say it's fine for the length of a shower or a little bit longer (maybe up to 20 minutes), so use the same rule here. Don't disconnect for longer than what your diabetes team recommends. Or your plan might involve leaving your pump on but keeping it in a place that won't get in the way.

Pregnancy

Another way that diabetes has something to do with sex is pregnancy. (Even if you are a teenage boy, it's good to read this section.) Obviously, sexual intercourse can lead to a girl becoming pregnant. A woman with diabetes who becomes pregnant will be watched very closely by her doctors. The reason for this is the mother's health will affect the developing baby's health. Also, because of hormonal changes, weight gain, and insulin resistance, blood sugars may be harder to control during pregnancy. Keeping blood sugars in tight control during pregnancy is very important. Women with diabetes who plan to get pregnant and work out all of the details with their doctors and nurses are more likely to have smooth pregnancies. Having diabetes does *not* mean that you should not get pregnant. It only means that you have an extra thing to think about and should work closely with your medical team while pregnant.

Putting It All Together

The bottom line is that you have to decide how comfortable you are engaging in sexual activity as a teen. This will depend on your beliefs and what you know about relationships and sex. In this chapter, you've learned that it's important to talk to your significant other about your diabetes and find ways to keep diabetes from getting in the way of your relationships. Plus, I hope you've learned that it is crucial to talk to your diabetes doctor and nurse when you're thinking about sexual activity or wanting protection or contraceptives. Because you have diabetes, your team can help you decide what's best for you and your body. It's important to keep all these things in mind as you get in to the next chapter about staying on track. As you get older and maybe move out on your own, get into more serious relationships, you'll need some strategies for staying on track with your diabetes. The next chapter covers that.

Chapter 11

Staying on Track

Great job getting through the first 10 chapters. We covered a lot and you may be on information overload at this point, but just a little bit more. This chapter reviews the main points of the book and shows you how to use them to stay on track. So, just where does this track lead? Well, it leads to a successful and happy life. Sure, it sounds a little cheesy and you may feel like that's a long way off, but you're already on the track. And trying the things listed in this book will keep you on that track. You'll feel healthier—physically and emotionally—and you'll get a lot more out of your life. So, let's dive right in.

Main Points

Three major points were made in this book:

1—Own your diabetes and make it a priority
2—Advocate for yourself
3—Prevent diabetes burnout

When you do these things, you'll be able to take good care of your diabetes, you won't feel like it's a nuisance, and you'll do well in a ton of other areas. Of course, it will take work by you (and support from the people around you), but you can do it. Here's how these three things keep you on track.

Own Your Diabetes

By owning your diabetes, you'll find that nice middle ground between really disliking diabetes and proclaiming your love for diabetes to the world. Okay, that's a little over the top, but you get the point. When you don't own your diabetes, you resent that you have it, you don't take care of it, and you use it as an excuse a lot. When you own it, you're going to be a lot more comfortable with yourself and around other people, and you'll have fewer embarrassing moments around diabetes. You'll look out for yourself and figure out ways that people on your support team can help. You'll be more responsible and reap the benefits of responsibility by getting to do more "grown-up" things. Here's how to own your diabetes and make taking care of it a priority in your life.

Get it out there. It usually feels good to talk about things, and that includes diabetes. You'll start to feel like you're fitting in better when you talk more about diabetes to the people around you. Also, you can learn more about diabetes on websites and from books and talk to other teens with diabetes online or in person, and then discuss those things with the people around you.

Take pride in your diabetes care. We're all really good at figuring out things that we are doing wrong and then being hard on ourselves about them. But you've got to notice the good things and pat yourself on the back. Tell your parent or doctor about the days that went very smoothly for your diabetes. Try to match up something fun (like going to a concert on a Wednesday) or something you really want (like extra cell phone minutes) with doing more checks. This becomes even more important as you get older and are on your own (with a new set of support team members). Remember to reward yourself and feel good about how well you're doing with your diabetes.

Advocate for Yourself

Being an advocate now, and in the future, gives you more control over what happens with your diabetes. It can make you feel more independent while also helping you understand who to ask for help, and what kind of help to ask for. Below is a review of how to be your own best advocate.

Know what you're talking about. Be informed. Educate yourself. For example, take an active interest in the types of insulin you're taking and whether different ways of giving insulin or checking blood sugars may work better for you. Read, talk to other teens, and ask your diabetes nurse and doctor for guidance.

Know how to say it. Get your point across by listening first, being prepared, and asking questions. Your doctor might ask you for your opinion on something she wants to change about your diabetes regimen. When you start seeing another diabetes doctor (as an adult), he may be a little more straightforward and direct with you. Be ready for this and know how to say what you want and need (more about this soon).

Compromise. We're talking about diabetes here, but this applies to every interaction you'll have with humans—be ready to compromise. Know what you're willing to give and not give on. Try to understand the other person's perspective and negotiate a compromise. It's not important for you to win, but rather, it's important to be sure everyone gets what they need and they're satisfied.

Prevent Diabetes Burnout

Here's our equation:

own your diabetes and make it a priority + advocate for yourself = prevent diabetes burnout

In other words, the first two steps keep diabetes burnout from creeping up. Diabetes burnout happens when the daily grind of checking blood sugars, giving injections (or boluses), and just dealing with having diabetes makes you feel overwhelmed and frustrated that things aren't better. Burnout leads to backing off and you end up not taking care of your diabetes the way you need to. So, in addition to the first two steps in our equation that can help to prevent diabetes burnout, here are other ways to battle diabetes burnout if it's already happening.

Pay attention to your feelings. Most of the warning signs of diabetes burnout are feelings. Feelings like frustration or anger. Or feeling annoyed or down. Try to figure out why you're feeling this way by connecting the dots. *I can't seem to control my blood sugars, I don't feel great, and my parents are on my back. Maybe that's why I'm feeling so annoyed with diabetes and wish I didn't have it.* If you are more aware of your feelings, you'll be better at battling burnout.

Do something about your feelings. There are a ton of options for you when these feelings come up. First, you can talk to a friend just to get it off your chest. Second, talk to your diabetes team and see if something can be changed to make it feel a little less stressful. Third, ask for help from family members or others on your support team. Finally, if you need to, talk to a therapist about how you're feeling. Diabetes burnout can lead to depression, so you've got to try to stop it before it gets really bad.

Control what you can. Can you make your A1c number go lower just by thinking about it? Nope, that won't happen. But you can control the things that affect your A1c. You can focus on what you're eating and maybe see a dietician to get on a better diet. You can control how much you exercise, even if it's only walking to and from school. You can control what you do about your blood sugars. Pick the parts to control, not what the end result is. In other words, focus on your diet or exercise instead of *I've got to get my A1c down!*

Control your thoughts. It's easy to fall in to the trap of thinking about how annoying diabetes is or constantly questioning what's going to happen to your body over time. If you focus too much on this, worry about it too much, you will stop doing things that remind you of these thoughts. You might stop going to the doctor as much. You might stop checking as much because a high blood sugar makes you think about getting complications down the road. Try to push out those negative thoughts or challenge them. You can use the problem solving strategy discussed in Chapter 5 (and reviewed next).

Have a good approach to solving problems. You can think of making decisions, challenging a negative thought, and many other things as problems you have to solve. Remember to identify the problem, brainstorm solutions, come up with the pros and cons of each solution, pick the best solution, and then see if it works.

Other Things That Keep You on Track

In addition to the three things just discussed, there are other things you can do to stay on track with your diabetes. And these things are also important for preventing or battling diabetes burnout.

Use Your Support Team

We discussed two types of support teams—your regular support team and your school support team. And you have team members on the essential and expanded rosters. Lots to keep track of, huh? Well, no matter who we are talking about, there are some basic things to keep in mind. These apply to talking to your diabetes doctor or nurse, a teacher at school, a parent, or a friend. You've got to find a way to get along with and get the kind of support you need from these team members. Here's how.

Focus on teamwork. You can try to take care of diabetes on your own, but it's going to be tough. You're much better off with teamwork. Be a teammate with your parent by sharing tasks. Be a teammate with your diabetes nurse by getting her the information she needs (blood sugars) so she can help you with what you need (to adjust insulin correctly and not have diabetes interfere with your fun activities). Be a teammate with a friend by talking about things that bother you...and things that make you really happy.

Follow the rules for teamwork. You're going to be part of a successful team if you are specific in your requests of others and do so in a respectful way. You may need to find some alternatives to talking if there's conflict that doesn't seem to go away. Perhaps you send texts, leave notes on a board on the fridge, or have a sibling help by talking for you. And reciprocate support. Do things for your teammates, as they are helping you.

Prepare for life changes. Now, it won't be long before you're an official adult. When you turn that magical age of 18, you become an adult and have all kinds of new rights. You're also going to start seeing "adult" doctors and nurses for your diabetes care. And you'll notice some differences. Your diabetes support team (doctor, nurse, dietician) will focus a lot more on how YOU are taking care of your diabetes. They may ask if you have help with certain things, but as an adult with diabetes, it is almost entirely your responsibility to take care of your diabetes. Does that make you a little nervous? Well, you've got time to get prepared for what it will be like. Use some of the same strategies like being prepared when you ask for things, be as specific as possible, and do a lot of work on your own to learn about new ways to manage diabetes.

Plus, you should still rely on your support team, even if the members change. Find ways to get those new friends to help with your diabetes management. If you're on a college campus, seek out other students with diabetes. Perhaps there's a group on campus for students with diabetes. If you're working right after high school, rely on some of the same people for support and seek out groups around town. You may meet someone who is managing diabetes in a way that's new to you (like a new device or insulin pump) and you want to learn more about it.

Be Informed, Be Prepared, Be Smart

This phrase pretty much applies to everything you do. But in this book, it pertains to alcohol and drugs, and romantic relationships and sex. You've got to know the facts before getting in to those things. Let's review a few things and then see how they will keep you on track with your diabetes.

Peer pressure is real, even if the facts aren't. Have you had someone say, "Come on, everyone's doing it," right before offering you a smoke? Even though that's a myth about alcohol and drug use—that everyone's doing it—that might not stop you from doing it. So, you've got to be prepared. If you're going to drink or use drugs, plan for it and be smart. Have someone sober with you who knows you have diabetes. Wear your medical ID bracelet and make sure your diabetes is in order before using. If you learn what can happen to your body because of diabetes and these substances, you'll be prepared and smart.

Romance and diabetes can mix. Diabetes can make it a little tougher to be intimate with someone. After all, there are needles, test strips, and tubing if you're on a pump. But this will all be easier if you're upfront with your date about your diabetes. Talk about it and help her (or him) understand. And like everything else, be prepared and smart. If you're focused on how embarrassing something might be because of diabetes and you forget to be safe (wear or make it mandatory for your partner to wear protection), that's a problem.

Give Yourself a Break

Finally, you've got to give yourself a break. It can be a lot of work—and hard work—to manage diabetes, so you've got to cut yourself some slack from time to time. Of course, everything in this book emphasizes ways to take better care of your diabetes and by doing that, you'll get much more enjoyment out of your life. However, your life can't be consumed by diabetes. If you notice that you're getting upset any time your blood sugar is even the least bit high or you're constantly on yourself about certain things that don't seem to be going well, take a break and evaluate how important that thing is. Sometimes we can pick up so much momentum with something that we can't stop it when it gets overwhelming. Like a snowball rolling down a hill that becomes bigger and bigger until it crushes a house at the bottom of the hill. You've got to find a balance. If you follow the tips and strategies in this book, and occasionally give yourself a break, you'll achieve that balance between work (on diabetes) and fun.

Putting It All Together

The rest of the book includes resources on websites you can visit, other books you and your support team members can read, and the nuts and bolts of taking care of diabetes. More information on the advantages and disadvantages of insulin pumps, technologies like continuous glucose monitoring, and other things are in the "nuts and bolts" section. But this is the final message of the book: You have the tools to manage diabetes and make it a seamless part of your life. You're not alone—there are a lot of us doing that out in the world. You don't have to be annoyed by diabetes and its management. And achieving all the things you want while taking great care of your diabetes will be even sweeter—now and in the future.

Section Three

Resources Galore

Chapter 12

The Nuts & Bolts of Type 1 Diabetes

This part of the book is intended to give you more information about taking care of your diabetes. Use this information to be a better advocate for yourself and make choices about the best way to manage your diabetes. This isn't all the information you need, but it's a start. Check out the Resources list for other places to get information. Let's start with what's expected of you as a teen with diabetes, then we'll discuss some of your options.

Expectations

Each year, the American Diabetes Association (ADA) publishes recommendations for how your diabetes support team is supposed to help you, and how you can help yourself take care of your diabetes. It's pretty long, so here are the basics.

Check Your Blood Sugars

According to the ADA, you should check your blood sugar at least 3–4 times a day. This helps to figure out if the amount of insulin you're getting is the right amount, what certain foods do to your blood sugars, and how to keep really low and high blood sugars from happening. Your diabetes team may ask you to check more and you might also want to check more because you've figured out that checking more helps keep your blood sugars in a tighter range. If you think about blood sugars as information and not as "good" or "bad", you'll probably check more. Try to get as much information as possible and don't get upset about them. (Remember talking about slowing your reaction time in Chapter 3?) Just use the information to decide what you need to do to get your blood sugar in the right range.

There are a ton of blood sugar meters that come in different sizes, colors, time it takes to do a check, and amount of memory to store blood sugars. You're more likely to check if you use one you like, whether you like it because of the color, size, or both. The Resources section (next) lists some websites you can visit to find out about different meters.

Take Insulin

You need to get insulin in to your body for one simple reason—your body's not making it anymore (or making very little of it). Insulin acts like a key that unlocks the parts of food and drinks that are needed to give you energy. Plus, insulin helps with bodily processes that happen throughout the day. Long-acting insulins are the *basal* part of a basal-bolus insulin regimen and they help with this stuff going on all the time. What's the name of the long-acting insulin you take? Lantus, Levemir, or maybe others?

Now, when you eat or drink something that has carbohydrates in it, insulin changes those carbs in to fuel for your body. But it's with a different type of insulin. The *bolus* part of basal-bolus is a fast-acting insulin and its primary job is to pull the "fuel" out of the food you eat. It works at the same time your food is being digested—that's why you try to take insulin at the same time you start eating (or before you start).

Are you on a basal-bolus regimen? It's popular because basal-bolus gives insulin in a way that matches what happens in the body of a person without diabetes, so you usually can keep your blood sugars in a tighter range. Basal-bolus is also popular because it gives you more flexibility for eating. You may not like eating lunch at the same time each day, and you may not always feel like having a snack. Basal-bolus allows you to do that—not eat or snack at the same times.

You can do basal-bolus with injections or a pump, but there are some unique parts to the pump that we will talk about in a minute. If you're doing basal-bolus with injections, you will probably take 1–2 injections a day of the basal insulin and 2–4 of the bolus insulin. So, you might take more injections in a day, but it's a more precise way of giving insulin and you have more flexibility.

Now, there's a chance you use NPH or R (regular) insulin. Those insulins are older and they are more like intermediate-acting insulins. They require you to eat and snack at certain times so you don't end up going low. You can be successful on these regimens, but it gives you less flexibility. Plus, they don't work the way that insulin works in a person without diabetes. So, you may want to see about doing a basal-bolus regimen if you're using NPH, R, or a mixed insulin. Talk to your doctor and nurse about it.

A "Good" A1c

All this talk about checking blood sugars, giving insulin, and paying attention to what you eat and how much exercise is important because it helps you take better control of your diabetes. You can tell how much control you have over your diabetes with the A1c value. Your A1c value shouldn't run your life, but you need to pay attention to it. So, just what is a good value? Well, the ADA recommends that teens (ages 13–19) keep their A1c around 7.5% or lower. For young adults (and all adults actually), the ADA recommends an A1c of 7.0% or lower. They make these recommendations because keeping it around those levels should keep you from getting complications or at least delay when they start.

Do you feel like you constantly hear from your diabetes support team that you've got to get your A1c down? Well, you're not alone. Most teens struggle to keep their A1c values around 7.5% or lower. As the book discussed, it's hard to do all the things you want to do as teen and take great care of your diabetes. But try the things in this book and see if your next A1c value is better. Don't be disappointed if the next one isn't that much better because your A1c value represents what has happened with your diabetes over the past 2–3 months. It takes a little bit of time to change your A1c. And remember, focus on the smaller things that lead to improving your A1c—things like exercising, eating a healthy diet, and checking blood sugars frequently.

Your Options

You have options for how you meet the expectations of checking blood sugars and taking insulin, and meeting your A1c goal. Work with your diabetes support team to figure out which options are best for you. You (and your parents) have to consider how much it costs and whether your insurance (or your parents' insurance) company will pay for these options. You've also got to think about the pros and cons of doing something new. Here are two examples.

Insulin Pump

Insulin pumps have been around for a long time, but are smaller and more precise now. The pump operates on a basal-bolus regimen. For the basal part, imagine a leaky faucet dripping every few seconds throughout the day. The insulin pump does the same thing—gives you small "drips" of insulin all the time. Now, the bolus part is the same as before—you give fast-acting insulin to match the food you're eating or to correct a high blood sugar. Instead of doing an injection, you're now pushing a button on the pump to give insulin.

So, what are the differences between doing basal-bolus on your pump versus doing it with injections? Well, the first major thing is that you're no longer doing injections (duh!). You have to change the pump cartridge that holds the insulin and insert the pump catheter (actually called a *cannula*) with a needle every two or three days, but that's the only "injection" you do. The little catheter and where you do it gets changed every two or three days because that's how long the insulin is good for in your pump.

If you can change your pump cartridge and add new insulin more frequently, like every two days, that might help your body use the insulin more efficiently. Some recent studies also found that changing it more frequently than every three days will help your blood sugars. The other reason to change the insulin in your pump and move the insertion site is so you don't get an infection. It's the same thing as injections—you've got to rotate where you do this on your body.

Another major difference is that you only have one insulin in your pump. It's always a fast-acting insulin. With your diabetes doctor and nurse, and your input, you program the pump to give this fast-acting insulin in very small doses throughout the day (like the drips). Because you do it that way, you're actually making it act like a long-acting insulin. And you program your pump and can put in different amounts of basal insulin throughout the day. Perhaps you need more insulin overnight than during the day. That's easy to program. You can also program different insulin to carb ratio at different times during the day. And when you need to eat or correct, the fast-acting part of the insulin is right there. You just punch in the dose like you would dial up insulin on a pen or fill a syringe.

Okay, so what are the disadvantages of using an insulin pump (and ways to overcome them)?

- You just might not like the idea of trusting a little computer to give you all your insulin. However, pumps are very reliable.
- You may not like being "connected" to something all the time. Well, you can take the pump off during showers, but you'll have it on the rest of the time. Some teens disconnect for high-contact sports (football, hockey) and you can't swim with it, but otherwise, it will be your little friend that's with you all the time.
- Wearing an insulin pump may make it undeniably clear to others that you have diabetes. Now, most of the book has talked about owning your diabetes and being open with people about it, but you still should be in control of how you do that. If someone sees the pump on you, they could ask questions or assume it's a pager or something else. There are ways to keep the pump hidden on your body. Guys can wear it on their belt loop (looks like a phone or pager) and while girls can too, if you're not wearing pants, you've got to get a little more creative. It is probably a bit easier for guys than girls when you're trying to disguise where the pump is on your body (if that's what you want to do).
- Pump supplies can cost more money. While the insulin pump offers a lot of flexibility and usually helps you bring down your A1c, the additional cost can be a concern. Some insurance companies may make it a little tough to get on it, but you should work with your diabetes team and call the company that makes the pump you want—they can usually help a lot, too. There are a number of pumps out there, so you should visit their websites and ask to see what they're like. The resources list has some of that information.

Continuous Glucose Monitoring

Another option is to use continuous glucose monitoring (CGM). What happens with CGM is that a small sensor is inserted under the skin (about the same size as the insulin pump cannula), and then the part above the skin is hooked up to a transmitter (about the size of a half-dollar coin). The sensor reads the level of glucose in the fluid under the skin and the transmitter sends that value to the device that displays the number. This device is about the size of a pump (or may actually be part of your pump). You can get a glucose reading every five minutes or about 300 readings a day.

Now, a fingerstick blood glucose check and a CGM reading are checking different things. Your fingerstick check picks up glucose in the blood. Your CGM picks up glucose in the interstitial fluid (fluid right under your skin). They are usually pretty similar, but fingerstick glucose changes before sensor glucose. Because of this, you still have to check your blood glucose and put that number in your device. That way, the readings you get on your CGM will better match the blood glucose. Are you confused yet? Well, this leads to a few things to think about when using CGM.

- You still have to check blood sugars. You may check less, the same, or more.
- You can't rely solely on the CGM readings to figure out what you should do about correcting high or low blood sugars. For example, if you're getting ready to give insulin or think you should correct a high glucose reading, you still need to do a fingerstick.
- You may have to wear two separate devices. A couple of companies have CGM that is incorporated in to the insulin pump, but others are separate.

But there are a number of advantages.

- You get information in real-time. You can see if your sensor glucose is going up quickly, down quickly, or changing a lot at different times of the day. You can see what happens when you eat certain foods or exercise.
- You can use that information to change basal rates in your pump (or doses and timing of insulin injections), with the help of your diabetes support team, of course.

- Most of the CGM devices also have software that you can use online to see exactly what happens across the day with your sensor glucose.
- Maybe most importantly, CGM devices have alarms. You can set these alarms when the readings are getting low. This can help a ton to keep you from having really low lows. It basically warns you that you're getting low and should do something about it. That's a nice thing.

Not all insurance companies pay for CGM and the ones that do may charge a little more than what you want to pay or can afford to pay. A lot of times you (or your parents) can work with your diabetes team to fill out forms that can help to get CGM approved. There are more and more people doing CGM and a lot of times, you can try it before you actually go on it. Definitely check to see if this is a good option for you.

Putting It All Together

Hopefully, this part of the book gave you a few ideas about what's expected of you in taking care of your diabetes as well as what options you have. Check with your diabetes support team, try things out, and find a diabetes regimen that fits you. Also, look over the Resources list (which is next) to get more information about some of these expectations and options.

Books, Organizations, & Websites

Books for Teens

Below is a select listing of books that I recommend. You can also find a slew of resources at the Children With Diabetes website. It lists different categories of books. Some are for you, others are for your parents. None are as good as the one you're reading (obviously!), but there are others that are good resources for you and your parents.

Burnout

Betschart, Jean, & Thom, Susan. (1995) *In Control: A Guide for Teens with Diabetes*. New York, NY: John Wiley & Sons.

Polonsky, William. (1999). *Diabetes Burnout: What to Do When You Can't Take It Any More*. Alexandria, VA: American Diabetes Association.

Health & Fitness

Colberg, Sheri. (2009). *Diabetic Athlete's Handbook*. Champaign, IL: Human Kinetics.

The Pump

Walsh, John, & Roberts, Ruth. (2006). *Pumping Insulin: Everything You Need For Success on a Smart Insulin Pump*. San Diego, CA: Torrey Pines Press.

Wolpert, Howard. (2002). *Smart Pumping: A Practical Approach to the Insulin Pump*. Alexandria, VA: American Diabetes Association.

Organizations & Websites

Each of these organizations (and websites) has extensive resources. You'll find quick fact sheets, forums on which you can talk to other teens with type 1 diabetes, and a host of other great information. Check them out—your parents will get good use out of these, too.

American Diabetes Association (ADA)

www.diabetes.org
www.diabetes.org/living-with-diabetes/parents-and-kids/planet-d/

The ADA website lists all kinds of statistics and information about diabetes. It is a good resource, but you'll be better off just going to the teen site if you're interested in chatting with other teens on the teen forum or getting teen-specific information. There is information there about taking diabetes to school and other important resources.

Centers for Disease Control and Prevention (CDC)

www.cdc.gov/healthyyouth/AdolescentHealth

This links you directly to the CDC's Healthy Youth website. You can click on different health topics and there is a ton of information on alcohol and drugs, nutrition, sex, as well as diabetes. The main part of the CDC's website also has information on diabetes causes and statistics. It may be a good resource if you're trying to help someone else learn more about diabetes.

Children With Diabetes

www.childrenwithdiabetes.com

This website has it all. There is information about diabetes in general, how to take care of it, and how to handle sports and other activities. Plus, there are forums where you can ask questions and talk to other teens with diabetes. Parents can also use this to chat with other parents of kids and teens with diabetes. There are also links for information about taking diabetes to college or taking care of diabetes at jobs. Different meters, insulin pumps, and types of insulin are also described and reviewed in the "Products" section.

dLife

www.dlife.com

This website is geared more toward adults, but has tons of information about diabetes. You can find different recipes, suggestions for selecting a blood sugar meter, and plenty of other things. There is an active forum to communicate with other individuals with diabetes, however, not much is happening on the teen support group site. (Teens may be at the other sites listed here.)

Juvenile Diabetes Research Foundation (JDRF)

www.jdrf.org
www.juvenation.org

The JDRF does a lot of work in local communities to help advocate for people with diabetes as well as running support groups. The main website has a lot of information about diabetes and research on finding a cure for diabetes. The Juvenation link has specific resources for teens and has opportunities to meet other teens within a social networking framework.

Additional Organizations

American Association of Diabetes Educators (AADE)

www.diabeteseducator.org

Either your nurse or your dietician, or someone you work with in the diabetes clinic, is a certified diabetes educator. This is the site for the association of diabetes educators. Information on this website ranges from information the professional would need to get certified as a diabetes educator (you might be interested in this type of job in the future) to videos about something called AADE7, which is a series of steps to help you manage your diabetes by yourself. This could be really helpful as you get older.

National Institute of Diabetes and Digestive and Kidney Diseases (NIDDK)

www.diabetes.niddk.nih.gov

The NIDDK is part of the National Institutes of Health (NIH) and they provide money to conduct different types of research—about the causes of diabetes, how people cope with diabetes, and other areas. There's lots of information here, too. You may want to use this website to learn more about what's going on right now with research on diabetes. Also, there's a link to the National Diabetes Education Program (NDEP), which has some really cool pieces to it that might help you manage your diabetes.

Acknowledgments

I want to thank all the teens and families who allowed me to be part of their lives. I hope I've done justice to the hard work you do to take care of your diabetes, day in and day out, by making this book helpful to other teens and families.

I have been fortunate to work with professionals in pediatric diabetes who demonstrate passion for what they do and dedication to the families with whom they work. Thanks to Suzanne Johnson for igniting my passion for work in diabetes. Thanks to Lori Laffel, Marilyn Ritholz, Debbie Butler, Alan Jacobson, Jamie Wood, Britta Svoren, Ann Goebel-Fabbri, Howard Wolpert, and the entire pediatric team at Joslin Diabetes Center for helping me learn so much and enjoy tremendously my time in Boston. Thanks to Barbara Anderson, Michael Harris, Jill Weissberg-Benchell, Tim Wysocki, Amanda Lochrie, and many others for opening doors and being the best collaborators anyone could ask for. Thanks to Denny Drotar, Larry Dolan, and my colleagues in the Adherence Center and the Diabetes Center at Cincinnati Children's for being enthusiastic, supportive, and dedicated to our current efforts to help children, teens, and their families. And thanks to the entire team at Magination Press, particularly Becky Shaw, for the hard work, dedication, insight, and enormous assistance that went in to the creation and production of this book.

Finally, I am very grateful to have the support of my family and friends. Thanks to Dawn, Maria, Morgan, Dad, Mom, Ryan, Abbe, Sandra, Keith, Chris, Jeremy, Brendan, Avani, Jamie, Jason, Sumit, Dorielle, Bryan, Michelle, and many others. You all contribute to an enjoyable life with diabetes.

About the Author

Korey K. Hood, PhD, has personal experience with diabetes. He was diagnosed with type 1 diabetes as a young adult. Coincidentally, it happened just a few months after starting graduate work in pediatric diabetes. Being diagnosed at this point in his life solidified the decision he made to do research and clinical work in pediatric diabetes and seemed to promote more enthusiasm for working in this area.

Dr. Hood's combination of education, career, and personal experiences in type 1 diabetes provide him with a unique perspective to engage teenagers with type 1 diabetes and attempt to promote their health and overall quality of life.

Dr. Hood completed his PhD in clinical and health psychology at the University of Florida, with a focus on pediatric and child clinical psychology, but the broad training included family work and individual work with adults with medical conditions.

Presently, Dr. Hood works at the Cincinnati Children's Hospital, where he is part of a newly developed center that focuses on promoting adherence and self-management in pediatric chronic disease. He works exclusively in type 1 diabetes and has active projects on the influence of psychological factors on diabetes management and interventions for depressed adolescents with type 1 diabetes.

About the Illustrator

Bryan Ische is an illustrator and designer currently living in Minneapolis, Minnesota. He graduated from the Minneapolis College of Art and Design (MCAD) in 2009 with a BFA in Illustration. He does his best to enjoy the things that come and try not to forget the things that pass.

About Magination Press

Magination Press publishes self-help books for kids and the adults in their lives. We are an imprint of the American Psychological Association, the largest scientific and professional organization representing psychologists in the United States and the largest association of psychologists worldwide.